SELF LEARNING OF BIOINFORMATICS ONLINE

By AJIT KUMAR ROY

The book is dedicated to my grand daughter
'ANGANA'

PREFACE

The idea of writing this book came as a result of over a decade long teaching, research and development activities in the field of Bioinformatics to fill the demand of students/researchers engaged in the field. With the arrival of genomics and genome sequencing projects, biology has been transformed into an incredibly data-rich science. The vast amount of information generated has made computational analysis critical due to lack of adequate skilled bioinformaticians. Therefore, the need for online learning has arisen. Many institutions all over the world started online courses. There are already thousands of online bioinformatics resources available. One of the limiting factors of the field is the difficulty in navigating the vast array of resources to identify the most appropriate tool for what you need to do.

The book explores ways that you can quickly find and effectively learn using online web resources. It includes a tour of example resources, organized by categories such as online tutorials, Practical, solutions, videos, blogs and social media covering algorithms and analysis tools, expression resources, genome browsers. One can learn how to find resources with the OpenHelix free search interface. OpenHelix searches hundreds of genomics resources, tutorial suites, and other material to deliver the most relevant resources in seconds.

Advent of the Internet and the rise of Web-based tools and technologies, resources, web content, blog posts, videos, webinars, and web sites that will facilitate easy access and use that saves time and effort avoiding massive generalized searches or hunting and pecking through lists of databases. The purpose of the book is to bridge the gap between the rising demand for self learning needs of biological and medical researchers and the availability online bioinformatics resources. A comprehensive list of online learning web tools, public sequence databases and open source software and technologies are provided. The book is divided into six chapters and within each chapter a number of weblinks added for quick access to desired material. This book focuses on latest online video repositories for educational and tutorial videos provided by resource developers and users along with blogs, twitter, face book discussions that in turn clarify so many unanswered questions.

It is a one-stop guided information gateway to the major bioinformatics databases and software, tools available freely on the Web. Over 3000 Web links on Practical lessons in the form of tutorials, videos, webinars, slides and Practical. Topics like search techniques with blast and psi-search to find homologous sequences in EMBL-EBI databases, input formats, how to change parameters and how to interpret the results. This also provides introduction to UNIPROT-GOA, the gene ontology annotation resource. An introduction to EMBL-EBI, UNICHEM - EMBL-EBI's mapping tool for small molecule database identifiers and European Nucleotide Archive (ENA) and data resources available. The links facilitates fundamental understanding on proteomics. genomics, metabolomics along with introductory knowledge for the beginners on topics like DNA & RNA, sequence alignment, gene expression, gene ontology, proteins, chemical biology, next generation sequencing, phylogenetics, proteins, structures, searching for structural homologues of a protein, how we can use UNIPROT to explore protein sequence and functional information.

Compiled by an expert, this practical book presents the most state-of-the-art bioinformatics applications with focuses on Comparative Genomics analysis, common DNA analysis tools, phylogenetics analysis, and SNP and haplotype analysis, microarray, SAGE, regulation of gene expression, miRNA, siRNA, and widely applied programs and tools in proteome analysis, protein sequences, protein functions, and functional annotation of proteins.

Following the book one can learn to find right and relevant online learning resources quickly, easily and how to use these independently, effectively and efficiently. It is an essential source of reference for high & secondary school, graduate & post graduate students in bioinformatics, computer science, mathematics, statistics, and biological sciences as current online resources and learning technologies will continue to impact bioinformatics education programs. The book is a compilation web resources developed by many educational institutions around the globe. Thanks are due to all those who originally conceived the idea of spreading the tools and techniques for the benefits of future generation of students and researchers.

AJIT KUMAR ROY

Contents

Chapter 1: TUTORIALS

Introduction

Bioinformatics is the application of computer technology to the management of biological information. The need for Bioinformatics has arisen from the recent explosion of publicly available genomic information, such as that resulting from the Human Genome Project. To address this, the National Center for Biotechnology Information (NCBI), at www.ncbi.nlm.nih.gov/, was established in 1988 as a national resource for molecular biology information. The NCBI creates public-access databases, develops software tools for analyzing genome data, and disseminates biomedical information - all for the better understanding of molecular processes affecting human health and disease. The NCBI is a virtual goldmine both in terms of available resources, and treasures yet to be discovered. Some of the many databases that the NCBI is responsible for include the Gene Bank DNA sequence databases, the Molecular Modeling Database (MMDB) consisting of three-dimensional protein structures, as well as tools for their visualization and comparative analysis; and the Online Mendelian Inheritance in Man (OMIM) database, which is a catalog of human genes and genetic disorders.

Source: (http://www.angelfire.com/ga2/nestsite2/bioinform.html)

A great place to start, whether you come from a biological, physical or computational background is at Martin Vingron's superb online bioinformatics tutorial (http://lectures. molgen.mpg.de/). (Begin by choosing a section from the left-hand-side menu bar.)

Tom Smith and Don Emmeluth have produced a nice little exploration (http://www.angelfire.com/ga2/nestsite2/bioinform.html) of bioinformatics using NCBI resources and tools.

A promising set of online lecture notes (http://www.genzentrum.lmu.de/) currently under construction by B. Steipe at the Genzentrum (Gene Center) (http://www.genzentrum.lmu.de/) at the Ludwig-Maximilians-Universität München (http://www.uni-muenchen.de/index.html) (University of Munich).

Chemistry for all: A defiantly frames-free chemistry tutorial site (http://dbhs.wvusd.k12.ca.us/Chem_Team Index.html).

Mathematics for biologists: First of all, an almost completely painless introduction (https://gitso-outage.oracle.com/thinkquest) to the horrors of the quadratic equation by Peter Whalen, James Walker, and Drew Marticorena.

C. J. Schwarz (http://people.stat.sfu.ca/~cschwarz/) of the Department of Statistics and Acturial Science (http://www.stat.sfu.ca/), Simon Fraser University (http://www.sfu.ca/) has produced a course in statistics which is accompanied by set of sound, online PDF handouts (http://people.stat.sfu.ca/~cschwarz/Stat-650/).

Here is a great guide (http://www.helsinkifi/~jpuranen/links.html) to a whole array of statistical learning/teaching resources prepared by Juha Puranen (http://www.helsinkifi/~jpuranen/) of the University of Helsinki (http://www.helsinki.fi/)[English(http://www.helsinki.fi/english/)].

Computers for biologists: Programming for biologists: General introduction to biology for computer scientists: Estrella Mountain Community College (http://www.emc.maricopa.edu/) in the States offers this excellent short introduction (http://www2.estrellamountain.edu/ faculty/farabee/BIOBK/BioBookintro.html) to biology (actually "The Nature of Science and Biology"). It's a great place for keyboard jockeys to start their journey to enlightenment.

Genetics: The Dolan DNA Learning Center at Cold Spring Harbor has an outstanding interactive tutorial (http://www.dnaftb.org/1/) introducing genetics. To take full advantage of the multimedia elements you should download the Flash (http://www.adobe.com/products/flashruntimes.html) and Real (http://www.real.com/) players.

Molecular biology for computer scientists: The Institute of Arable Crop Research Beginner's Guide to Molecular Biology (http://www.rothamsted.bbsrc.ac.uk/notebook/courses/guide/).

Protein chemistry for computer scientists: Unilever Education Advanced Series tutorial on proteins (http://www.schoolscience.co.uk/ content/5/chemistry/proteins/ index.html).

Cell biology for computer scientists: The University of Arizona (http://www.arizona.edu/) has made available a high-quality tutorial in cell biology (http://www.biology.arizona.edu/cell_bio/cell_bio.html). Not only does it cover the facts, but it also attempts to introduce some of the philosophy of the field---recommended. Even better, it's also available *en Español* (http://www.biologia.arizona.edu/cell/cell.html) and *in Italiano* (http://www.biologia-it.arizona.edu/cell_bio/cell_bio.html).

Once you've worked your way through that you might like to see some scanning electron microscope images (http://www.heuserlab.wustl.edu/v2.0/images/galleries/index.shtml) of some of the structures you've read about taken by members of John Heuser's lab (http://www.heuserlab.wustl.edu/v2.0/heuser-cv.shtml).

Evolution for computer scientists: Bob Patterson maintains his "Darwiniana" (http://hometown.aol.com/darwinpage/) with amazing diligence.

Practical Bioinformatics: Other lists of Bioinformatics Tutorials: More Tutorials Websites

(http://spdbv.vital-it.ch/TheMolecularLevel/Matics/)

(http://www.mrc-lmb.cam.ac.uk/rlw/text/bioinfo_tuto/ introduction.html)

(https://genome.ucsc.edu/training.html)

(http://mendel.informatics.indiana.edu/~yye/lab/teaching/fall2011-I519.php)

(https://www.bits.vib.be/index.php/training/122-basic-bioinformatics)

(imp basic concept: https://www.bits.vib.be/index.php/training/ 122-basic-bioinformatics)

Imp-Bioinfo-Solutions: (http://www.thebioinformatica.com/onlinetutorial.htm)

Dummies: (http://spdbv.vital-it.ch/TheMolecularLevel/Matics/)

> **BioMedNet Research Tools:** (http://research.bmn.com/)

> **CMS Molecular Biology Resource:** (http://mbcf.dfci.harvard.edu/cmsmbr/)

> **Genetics Tutorials:** (http://science.nhmccd.edu/biol/genetics.html)

> **Health Web/Genetics:** (http://healthweb.org/browse.cfm?subjectid=42)

> **Morgan--GeneticTutorial:** (http://morgan.rutgers.edu/ morganWebFrames/How_to_use/HTU_Frameset.html)

> **Online Mendelian Inheritance in Men (NCBI):** (http://www.ncbi.nlm.nih.gov/ sites/entrez?db=nucleotide)

> **Protein Information Resource:** (http://pir.georgetown.edu/)

> **Talking Glossary of Genetic Terms:** (http://www.genome.gov/glossary.cfm)

> **WWW Virtual Library-Genetics:** (http://www.ornl.gov/sci/techresources/Human_ Genome/genetics.shtml)

Foundation Tutorials for Bioinformatics Aspirants: Computer Tutorials for Science Stream Students

Introduction to computer Concepts:

> a) (www.compume.com)

> b) (www.grassrootsdesign.com)

> c) (www.fayette.k12.il.us)

d) (www.glencoe.com)

e) (www.comedition.com)

f) (www.hitmill.com)

g) (www.pstcc.cc.tn.us)

Introduction to Internet:

a) (http://oac3.hsc.uth.tmc.edu/staff/snewton/tcp-tutorial/)

b) (http://www.cisco.com/)

c) (http://www.ch.embnet.org/bio-www/archive/   florianW3_1.html)   or
(http://www.ch.embnet.org/ error.html)

HTML Tutorials:

a) (www.htmlgoodies.com/)

b) (www.bfree.on.ca)

c) (www.pagetutor.com)

d) (www.davesite.com)

e) (www.webreference.com)

f) (www.pageresource.com)

g) (http://www.devry-phx.edu)

h) (http://www.ncsa.uiuc.edu)

i) (http://www.w3.org/)

j) (http://archive.ncsa.uiuc.edu)

Java Tutorials:

a) (java.sun.com/docs/books/tutorial/) (http://docs.oracle.com/javase/tutorial/)

b) (http://www.oracle.com/technetwork/java/index.html)

c) (javaboutique.internet.com/tutorials/)

d) (www.freewarejava.com/tutorials/index.shtml)

e) (www.javacoffeebreak.com/tutorials/)

f) (www.apl.jhu.edu/~hall/java/FAQs-and-Tutorials.html)

g) (http://www.javaworld.com/)

Perl Tutorials:

a) (www.devdaily.com/perl/)

b) (www.pageresource.com/cgirec/index2.htm)

c) (www.perl.com/pub/q/resources)

d) (www.perlmonks.org)

e) Perl for Biologists (Weizmann Institute) (http://www.uni-hohenheim.de/~rebhan/perl/)

f) (www.webknowhow.net/dir/Perl/Tutorials/)

g) Perl for Biologists (http://www.mrc-lmb.cam.ac.uk/genomes/jong/perl_bio_book.html)

h) (savage.net.au/Perl-tutorials.html)

i) Welcome to the Bioperl Project ! (http://www.techfak.uni-bielefeld.de/bcd/Perl/Bio/welcome.html)

XML Tutorials:

a) (www.w3schools.com)

b) (www.zvon.org)

c) (www.xmlfiles.com)

d) (http://wdvl.internet.com/)

e) (www.finetuning.com)

SQL Tutorials:

a) (www.sqlcourse.com/)

b) (www.w3schools.com/sql/default.asp)

c) (www.sqlcourse2.com/)

d) (php.weblogs.com/sql_tutorial)

e) (perl.about.com/cs/beginningsql/)

f) (www.db.cs.ucdavis.edu/teaching/sqltutorial/)

Oracle Tutorials:

a) (www.hot-oracle.com/)

b) (www.oraclepower.com/)

c) (www.oraclepower.com)

d) (www.orafaq.org/suptutor.htm)

e) (www.vb-bookmark.com/OracleTutorial.html)

C & C++ Tutorials:

a) (www.cyberdiem.com/vin/learn.html)

b) (www.webwareindex.com/tutorials/C.html)

c) (www.cprogramming.com/tutorial.html)

d) (www.gustavo.net/programming/c__tutorials.shtml)

e) (http://www.dmoz.org/Computers/Programming/Languages/C/FAQs%2C_Help%2C_and_Tutorials/)

CGI Tutorials:

a) (www.htmlgoodies.com/beyond/cgi.html)

b) (www.cgi-resources.com/Documentation/CGI_Tutorials/)

c) (www.gustavo.net/programming/cgi.shtml)

d) (www.cgidir.com/Tutorials/)

e) (webdesign.about.com/cs/cgi/)

f) (http://www.cgi101.com/class/)

Visual Basic Tutorials:

a) (www.imt.net/~joe/matt/program/vb/Tutorials/)

b) (visualbasic.about.com/)

c) (visualbasic.ittoolbox.com/)

d) (members.tripod.com/~vkliew/vb.html)

e) (www.developerfusion.com/)

UNIX / Linux Tutorials:

a) (www.ee.surrey.ac.uk/Teaching/Unix/)

b) (webreference.com/programming/Unix/)

c) (www.uwsg.iu.edu/uhelp/tutorials/toc.html)

d) (www.unixtools.com/tutorials.html)

e) (www.networkcomputing.com/unixworld/ archives/tutorials.html)

f) (www.unix-manuals.com/)

g) (http://www.isu.edu/departments/comcom/unix/workshop/unixindex.html)

h) (http://www.ee.surrey.ac.uk/Teaching/Unix/)

i) (http://www.linuxnewbie.org/)

Science Tutorials for Computer Stream Students

Introduction to Biology:

    a) (scidiv.bcc.ctc.edu)

    b) (library.thinkquest.org/12413/)

    c) (www.biology-online.org/tutorials/home.htm)

    d) (www.lsic.ucla.edu/ls3/tutorials/)

    e) (biology-online.org/)

    f) Cartoon Guide to Genetics
        (http://www.amazon.com/exec/obidos/ASIN/0062730991/
        o/qid=957735943/sr=2-1/103-6986286-3259052)

    g) (genomebiology.com/tutorials/)

    h) (http://biomed.nus.sg/HIS/txt/menu/tacmenu.html)

    i) Tutorials in Molecular Biology (http://locutus.lsic.ucla.edu/ls3/tutorials/)

    j) (http://www.iacr.bbsrc.ac.uk)

    k) (http://gened.emc.maricopa.edu/Bio/BIO181/BIOBK/BioBookgloss.html)   -
        BioBook Glossary

    l) (http://highveld.com) - Internet Directory of Biology and Biotechnology

    m) (http://esg-www.mit.edu:8001/esgbio/7001main.html) - ESG Biology Hyper-
        textbook Home Page)

    n) (http://web.ornl.gov/sci/techresources/Human_Genome/redirect.shtml) - DOE
        Primer on Molecular Genetics)

Introduction to Chemistry:

    a) (www.chemistrycoach.com/tutorial.htm)

    b) (http://users.rcn.com/bobsalsa/tutorial.htm)

    c) (lrc-srvr.chemistry.ohio-state.edu/under/chemed/ chemed.htm)

    d) (http://www.unm.edu/~dmclaugh)

    e) (http://www.chem.umr.edu)

    f) (http://www.chem.umr.edu/Organic/index.html?organic+chemistry)

    g) (http://turner.lamf.uwindsor.ca)

    h) (http://www.chem.vt.edu)

    i) Periodic table of the elements - (http://pearl1.lanl.gov/periodic/)

    j) Interactive periodic table of the elements - (http://www.chemicalelements.com/)

Introduction to Biochemistry:

   a) (www.biology.arizona.edu/biochemistry/biochemistry.html)

   b) (www.umanitoba.ca/faculties/medicine/biochem/tutorials/)

   c) (www.ahpcc.unm.edu/~aroberts/main/ biochemistry_tutorials.htm)

   d) (www.massey.ac.nz/~wwbioch/Prot/tutehome/tutepage.htm)

   e) (http://xray.bmc.uu.se/Courses/Bke1/Tutorials/Tutorialindex.html)

   f) (http://www.jonmaber.demon.co.uk/)

About DNA:

   a) (http://biog-101-104.bio.cornell.edu/BioG101_104/   tutorials/recomb_DNA.
      html)

   b) (http://avery.rutgers.edu/WSSP/Tutorials/) (chime plug-in required)

   c) (www.umass.edu/molvis/freichsman/)

   d) (www.tutorgig.com/showurls.jsp?group=6732&index=0)

   e) (www.scientific.org/tutorials/articles/riley/riley.html)

   f) (www.tulane.edu/~biochem/nolan/lectures/rna/intro.htm)

   g) (http://lenti.med.umn.edu/recombinant_dna/recombinant_flowchart.html)

   h) DNA tutorial (http://www.101science.com/dna.html)

   i) DNA from the beginning (http://www.dnaftb.org/)

   j) Central Dogma Glossary (http://homepage.smc.edu/ hodson_kent/Dictionary/
      Glossary.htm)

About RNA:

   a) (www.imsb.au.dk/~raybrown/)

   b) (http://zombie.imsb.au.dk/~raybrown/)

   c) (ndbserver.rutgers.edu/NDB/structure-finder/tutorials/full_ndb.dna.rna.res.html)

About Genome:

   a) (http://genomebiology.com/tutorials/)

   b) (http://www.genomeweb.com/)

   c) (http://anatomy.med.unsw.edu.au/cbl/GENOME/tutorials.htm)

   d) (http://rsat.ulb.ac.be/rsat/tutorials/tut_genome-scale-patser.html)

   e) (home.uchicago.edu/~ebetran/guides.html)

f) Basic Genome Glossary - (http://www.nytimes.com/library/national/science/062600sci-genome-glossary.html)

g) Limited Genome Glossary - (http://homepage.smc.edu/hodson_kent/Dictionary/Glossary.htm)

h) Genome Glossary - (https://gitso-outage.oracle.com/ thinkquest)

i) The Gene-School Glossary (https://gitso-outage.oracle.com/thinkquest)

j) Glossary of Genetic Terms (http://www.nhgri.nih.gov/DIR/VIP/Glossary/)

Bioinformatics Tutorials

Useful Resource to Self-Study Bioinformatics(https://www.biostars.org/p/56401/

Introduction to Bioinformatics

1) Bioinformatics (Genomics) (http://post.queensu.ca/~forsdyke/bioinfor.htm)

2) Biocomputing in a Nutshell. (http://www.techfak.uni-bielefeld.de/bcd/ForAll/Basics)

3) Biologist's Guide to Internet Resources

4) Computational Molecular Biology Course (http://cmb.washington.edu/)

5) Course on Bioinformatics (http://www.cbi.pku.edu.cn/Doc/)

6) EMBNet Biocomputing Tutorials (http://www.hgmp.mrc.ac.uk/Embnetut/Universi/embnettu.html)

7) Finding the genes in the genomic sequences (http://helpdesk.ugent.be/webhosting/rugac.php)

8) The Genetic Programming Tutorial (http://geneticprogramming.com/)

9) Jose R. Valverde's training course documents (http://www.es.embnet.org/ Doc/)

10) Principles of Computational Biology, Steven Salzberg. (http://www.cs.jhu.edu/~salzberg/cs439.html)

11) Principles of Protein Structure Using the Internet (http://www.cryst.bbk.ac.uk/PPS2/course/)

12) Practical Course "Bioinformatics: Computer Methods in Molecular Biology" (http://www.icgeb.trieste.it/net/courses/bioinfo98.html)

13) Sequence analysis course (José R, Valverde, EMBNet/CNB) (http://www.es.embnet.org/Doc/ECJ/ ECJ-1999-01/coursecnb/)

14) Bioinformatics (http://post.queensu.ca/~forsdyke/ bioinfor.htm) - An excellent review on genetic code and information processing

15) Molecular Sequence Analysis (http://www.sequenceanalysis.com/) - Introductory sequence analysis by Andrew S Louka

16) Homology Modelling (http://swift.embl-heidelberg.de/course/) - Protein and homology modeling for beginners

17) Biocompanion (http://www.doelz.com/) - Tutorial for sequence analysis

18) Bioinformatics and Genomic Analysis (http://www.blc.arizona.edu/courses/bioinformatics/) - Link to graduate student course at the university of Arizona

19) EMBnet Biocomputing Tutorials - Introduction (http://www.hgmp.mrc.ac.uk/Embnetut/Universl/index. html)

20) Integrative Bioinformatics: Practical Kinetic Modeling of Biological Systems (http://www.bioinformaticsservices.com/bis/resources/cybertext/IBcont.html)

21) Biocomputing For Everyone ! (http://www.techfak.uni-bielefeld.de/bcd/ForAll/welcome.html)

22) The Biocomputing Glossary (http://www.cryst.bbk.ac.uk/BCD/ bcdgloss.html)

23) Computational Biology Course, Martin Tompa (http://courses.cs. washington.edu/courses/cse527/00wi/)

24) Course Distance Learning in Bioinformatics (http://130.88.90.2:8900/)

25) Functional genomics glossaries (http://ihome.cuhk.edu.hk/~b400559/ glossaries.html)

26) How to become a bioinformatics expert (http://www.techfak.uni-bielefeld.de/bcd/ForAll/Econom/study.html)

27) Internet for biologists (http://biobase.dk/Embnetut/Ifb/ifb_intr.html)

28) Jose R. Valverde's 'dirty' training course documents (http://www.es.embnet.org/Doc/Training/)

29) Algorithms in Molecular Biology (University of Washington) (http://www.cs.washington.edu/education/cources/590bi/98w/)

30) Protein Sequence Analysis in the Genomic Era (http://lipid.biocomp.unibo.it/school/)

31) Protein sequence and structure analysis : A practical guide. (http://www.biochem.ucl.ac.uk/bsm/dbbrowser/jj/)

32) Topics of Evolutionary Computation
(http://www.evalife.dk/index.php?lefturl=/eacourse2000/
topicsofEC2000.php)

33) VSNS BioComputing Division (http://www.techfak.uni-bielefeld.de/bcd/welcome.html)

34) Bioinformatics (http://twod.med.harvard.edu/seqanal/ index.html) - Primer on bio-sequence comparisons

35) Algorithms in Molecular Biolgy (http://www.math. tac.ac.il/~rshamir/algmb/algmb98.html) - Excellent for learning basics about many bioinfo tools

36) Biocomputing (http://www.hgmp.mrc.ac.uk/Embnetut/ Universi/embnettu.html) - Bio-computing tutorial at EBI

37) Bioinforamtics Training Resources
(http://www.med.nyu.edu/customerror/404) - Links to an excellent selection of bioinformatics tools training at NYU

38) DNA composition and Exon prediction (http://www. pdg.cnb.uam.es/cursos/FVi2001/GenomAna/ GeneIdentification/SearchContent/main.html) - Sequence based measures indicative of protein-coding function in genomic DNA

39) BCD BioComputing Tutorial (http://www.techfak.uni-bielefeld.de/bcd/Curric/welcome.html)

More Bioinformatics Tutorials

(http://beckerinfo.net/bioinformatics/bioinformatics-tutorials-2/): There are a number of great tutorials on the web for bioinformatics-related applications and topics. Bioinformatics Tutorials Series (BITS) from Count Way Library of Medicine at Harvard are on the following topics.

Bioinformatics (http://beckerinfo.net/bioinformatics/category/bioinformatics/)

BLAST (http://beckerinfo.net/bioinformatics/category/blast/)

database (http://beckerinfo.net/bioinformatics/category/database/)

EBI (http://beckerinfo.net/bioinformatics/category/ebi/)

Education (http://beckerinfo.net/bioinformatics/category/education/)

Ensembl (http://beckerinfo.net/bioinformatics/category/ensembl/)

genome (http://beckerinfo.net/bioinformatics/category/genome/)

genome browser (http://beckerinfo.net/bioinformatics/category/ genome-browser/)

helpful (http://beckerinfo.net/bioinformatics/category/helpful/)

informatics (http://beckerinfo.net/bioinformatics/category/ informatics/)

Information (http://beckerinfo.net/bioinformatics/category/ information/)

NCBI (http://beckerinfo.net/bioinformatics/category/ncbi/)

resources (http://beckerinfo.net/bioinformatics/category/resources/)

sequence (http://beckerinfo.net/bioinformatics/category/sequence/)

tool (http://beckerinfo.net/bioinformatics/category/tool/)

tutorial (http://beckerinfo.net/bioinformatics/category/tutorial/)

webinar (http://beckerinfo.net/bioinformatics/category/webinar/)

Other Tutorials

1) (http://spdbv.vital-it.ch/TheMolecularLevel/Matics/)

2) (http://www.mrc-lmb.cam.ac.uk/rlw/text/bioinfo_tuto/ introduction.html)

3) (https://genome.ucsc.edu/training.html)

4) (http://mendel.informatics.indiana.edu/yye/lab/teaching/fall2011-I519.php)

5) (https://www.bits.vib.be/index.php/training/122-basic-bioinformatics)

6) (imp basic concept: https://www.bits.vib.be/index.php/ training/122-basic-bioinformatics)

Virtual Online Tutorials

1) Virtual Institute of Bioinformatics (http://www.bioinf.org/ vibe/index.html) - **National University of Ireland**

2) UNIX, GCG, SEQLAB and STADEN Tutorials (http://www.molbiol.ox.ac.uk/tutorials.shtml) - Oxford University, UK

3) BIOTOOLS96 (http://www.vsms.nottingham.ac.uk/vsms/biotools/index.html) - (University of Nottingham, UK, Virtual school of molecular sciences

4) the principles of protein structure, using the internet (http://www.cryst. bbk.ac.uk/PPS2/top.html) - Birkback College (University of London), UK

5) Free online bioinformatics courses! s-star.org (http://s-star.org/main.htm)

6) Science and technology directory (http://www.technolgy-resource.co.uk/)

7) Weizmann Institute of Science Genome and Bioinformatics (http://www.bioinfo.wizmann.ac.il/bioinfo.html)

8) Algorithms for Molecular Biology (http://www.cs.tau. ac.il/~shamir/algmb.html) - Bioinformatics course notes, Tel Aviv University (TAU, Israel)

9) Certificate Program in Bioinformatics (http://scpd. stanford.edu/home) - Stanford

10) Courses Offered by BU Bioinformatics Program (http://engpub1.bu.edu/bioinfo/course.html)

11) ISCB Training information (http://www.iscb.org/training.html)

12) Penn Database Research Group- Classes (http://www.db.cis.upenn.edu/ Classes/)

13) VSNS Biocomputing Division (http://www.techfak.uni-bielefeld.de/bcd/ welcome.html)

14) Yale Bioinformatics -- Courses and Lectures (http://bioinfo.mbb.yale.edu/ lectures/)

15) Bioinformtics Online lecture (I) (http://lectures.molgen.mpg.de/)

16) Bioinformtics Online lecture (II) (http://www. genzentrum.lmu.de/) or (http://www.Imb.uni-muenchen.de/groups/bioinformatics/bioifo.html)

17) MRes Biomolecular Sciences Lecture Notes: 1. The Gene and Bioinformatics (http://www.hgmp.mrc.ac.uk/ ~dcounsel/MRes/MRes.html)

18) MRes Biomolecular Sciences Lecture Notes: 2. The Gene and Bioinformatics

19) biocomputing on internet (http://www.techfak.uni-bielefeld.de/bcd/ welcome.html) (University of) Bielefeld, Germany Virtual School of Natural Sciences

20) Sequence comparison (http://www.dir.univ-rouen.fr/~charras/seqcomp/) Universite de Rouen, France

21) A Guide to Molecular Sequence Analysis (http://www.sequenceanalysis.com/) National Hospital University of Oslo, Norway

22) Distant homologies: motifs, patterns, profiles (http://www.icgeb.trieste.it/net/courseware/Tiotle.htm) International Centre for Genetic Engineering and Biotechnology , Trieste, Italy

23) Virtual School of Natural Sciences BioComputing Division (http://merlin. mbcr.bcn.tme.edu:8001/bcdusa/ welcome.html) - Virtual bio-computing course

24) Algorithms for Computational Biology (Advanced Topics #6, 236606) (http://bioinfo.cs.technion.ac.il/) - Israel Institute of Technology

25) CSE 590BI (http://www.cs.washington.edu/education/ courses/590bi/) - Computational Biology, University of Washington

26) MBB 447b3 (747b3) Classes (http://bioinfo.mbb.yale. edu/course/classes/) - Yale

27) UCSC School of Engineering- Class Home Pages (https://courses.soe.ucsc.edu/classes/) - University of California at Santa Cruz

28) Virtual Bioinformatics Distance Learning (http://protein.uta.fi/bioinfo_courses) - Bioinformatics and Functional genomics courses offered by IMC Bioinformatics, University of Tampere

29) Tutorials using NCBI Bioinformtics Tools (http://www.angelfire.com/ga2/nestsite2/bioinform.html)

Free online training from GeneGo

(http://beckerinfo.net/bioinformatics/free-online-training-from-genego-july-dates/): Knowledge mining GeneGo content, EZ Search and MetaSearch Tired of spending hours searching the public domain building your research objectives? GeneGo now provides a new Google-like interface to search your favorite gene, protein, disease or compound with just one click. In this you will find details about expression (http://beckerinfo.net/bioinformatics/category/ expression/), genomics (http://beckerinfo.net/bioinformatics/category/genomics/), Information (http://beckerinfo.net/bioinformatics/category/information/), tutorial (http://beckerinfo.net/bioinformaticscategory/tutorial/), webinar (http://beckerinfo.net/ bioinformatics/category/webinar/).

Train online with EMBL-EBI(http://www.ebi.ac.uk/training/online/)

Online Courses: The educational institutions listed below have submitted information on their bioinformatics related online courses. To post an online course offered by your institution please use this form.

Focus	Course Title	University/Institution
Bioinformatics	Bioinformatics for transcriptomics	The University of Manchester

Focus	Course Title	University/Institution
Computational Biology	Bioinformatics for Systems Biology	University of Manchester
Math/Statistics	Mathematics for metabolic modelling	University of Manchester
Math/Statistics	Statistics and R for the Life Sciences	HarvardX
Bioinformatics	Advanced sequence analysis	The University of Manchester
Bioinformatics	Network Analysis in Systems Biology	Mount Sinai
Math/Statistics	Networks and Systems	East Tennessee State University
Bioinformatics	Bioinformatics Algorithms (Part 1)	University of California, San Diego
Bioinformatics	Perl and Unix for Bioinformatics	PerlSource Informatics
Bioinformatics	Perl for Biologists, Level 1	Bioinformatics.Org

Source: https://www.iscb.org/online-courses

Chapter 2: WEB TUTORIALS, TOOLS, AND RESOURCES

Web Tutorials

There are thousands of bioinformatics and genomics resources that are free and publicly accessible. However, trying to find the right resource for your need, and learn how to use the often complex features and functions can be difficult. The chapter explores ways that you can quickly find and effectively learn how to use resources. It will include a tour of example resources, organized by categories such as Algorithms and Analysis tools, expression resources, genome browsers (General, Eukaryotic and Prokaryotic/Microbial), Literature and text mining resources, and resources focused on nucleotides, proteins, pathways, disease and variation. At the end of the chapter, you'll learn how to find resources with the Open Helix **free search interface** (http://www.openhelix.com/index.shtml), learning to use resources with Open Helix **tutorials** (http://www.openhelix.com/cgi/tutorials.cgi) and a discussion of additional methods of learning about resources.

You'll learn:

    i. about several bioscience resources in various subject categories

    ii. to find the right resource using the Open Helix search interface

    iii. how to quickly learn to use resources through Open Helix tutorials,

    iv. site documentation, mailing lists, etc.

    v. about additional resources for discovering resources to meet your research needs

Find, Learn, and Deliver

Find the most relevant resource quickly and easily: Open Helix searches hundreds of genomics resources, tutorial suites, and other material to deliver the most relevant resources in seconds. Search at Open Helix saves time and effort--avoid massive generalized searches or hunting and pecking through lists of databases. With a subscription, you'll be able to access all the Open Helix training materials delivered in search results.

Learn how to use the resource: Save time and money with a subscription to nearly 100 Open Helix online tutorial suites:

    i. You can independently, effectively and efficiently learn to use a resource.

    ii. You and your staff can save time for your critical needs by relying on Open Helix tutorials to provide the introductory training on resources.

    iii. You and your institution save time and money when teaching others by using the provided PowerPoint slides, suggested script, slide handouts, and exercises.

Deliver breakthrough research: More efficient use of the most relevant resources means quicker and more effective research. With a subscription, you and your institution can further enable breakthrough research. You can deliver Open Helix tutorial suites within your already existing information portal or through the Open Helix site.

The most effective and efficient way to leverage genomics resources

    i. Quickly learn how to use a resource when you need it

    ii. Have a reference and teaching resource at your fingertips

    iii. Know you'll be using the most proven-effective training available

    iv. Have the confidence you have the best, most updated information

    v. Have peace of mind you are using materials created by experts

Quickly learn how to use a resource when you need it - The 30-60 minute online narrated tutorials, which run in just about any browser, highlight and explain all the features and functionality needed to start using the resource effectively. The tutorials also include a "movie," which walks the user through a sample exercise while the narrator explains and completes each step. Use the tutorial to introduce yourself to a new resource, to view new features and functionality, or simply as a reference tool to refresh your memory of the resource.

Have a reference and teaching resource at your fingertips - In addition to the tutorials, you also receive useful training materials (http://openhelix.com/cgi/subscriptions.cgi?tab=3) which can save time and effort to create classroom content.

Know you'll be using the most proven-effective training available - You will get the most effective and efficient way to learn how to use genomic resources. Online learning has proven to be as effective as on-site training for genomics resources, with the added benefit of lower cost and convenient any-time access.

Have the confidences you have the best, most updated information - Open Helix updates its tutorial suites as the resources change, and add new tutorials suites all the time.

Have peace of mind you are using materials created by experts - Open Helix has been providing training on genomics resources for over six years. Open Helix trainers all have PhDs in biological sciences, intimate knowledge of the resources, and have years of experience with on-site and online training. You can trust Open Helix expertise since many of the top resource provider's contract with Open Helix to provide their outreach and training.

Invaluable access to time saving content

An OpenHelix subscription gives you complete access to a catalog of 100 tutorial suites (http://www.openhelix.com/cgi/tutorials.cgi) in a wide range of categories (http://www.openhelix.com/cgi/ tutorialCategory.cgi). The breadth and depth of the resources covered assures you'll have the tutorial suite on the resources you need to learn Each Tutorial Suite includes (see an example with one of our sponsored tutorial suites - http://www.openhelix.com/cgi/freeTutorials.cgi):

    i. An **online narrated tutorial**, which runs in just about any browser, can be viewed from beginning to end or navigated using chapters and forward and backward sliders. The 30-60 minute tutorials highlight and explain all the features and functionality needed to start using the resource effectively. The tutorials also include a "movie," which walks the user through a sample exercise while the narrator explains and completes each step.

    ii. Complete **PowerPoint slide set** with animations and suggested script.

    iii. **Step-by-step exercises** for hands-on experience.

    iv. PDF of slides for **handouts**

    v. Access to all **new and updated tutorial suites**.

In addition to the subscription, all Open Helix users have the advantage of:

    a) Using the OpenHelix **Search** function to quickly find and access the training materials you need.

    b) Access to hundreds of brief video tips on features and functions of bioinformatics tools with the **OpenHelix blog** (http://blog.openhelix.com/) "tip-of-the-week" feature.

    c) The **OpenHelix Newsletter** (http://www.openhelix.com/ cgi/seminars.cgi?tab=5) giving you information on bioinformatics tools and resources, resource news, and updates on new and updated tutorials.

Washington University, USA

(http://www.openhelix.com/cgi/createAccount.cgi)

List of all Open Helix Tutorials: This is the full list of tutorials offered by OpenHelix. Clicking on a tutorial name will display detailed information, together with a list of all available training materials. To get a list of all tutorials in a particular category, click on the category name or display all tutorials grouped by category (http://www.openhelix.com/cgi/tutorialCategory.cgi).

Table: List of all Open Helix Tutorials

	Name	Description	Category	Resources
	Allen Mouse Brain Atlas	Mapped gene expression data in mouse brain	Expression	Allen Mouse Brain Atlas
	Alternative Splicing and Transcript Diversity (ASTD) database	A bioinformatics resource for alternative splice events and transcripts for human, mouse, and rat	Expression, Nucleotides, EBI	ASTD
	ArrayExpress	A public repository for microarray gene expression data at the EBI	Expression, EBI	ArrayExpress
	BiologicalNetworks	Analyze and visualize molecular interaction networks	Ye Olde Tutorials	BiologicalNetworks
	BioMart	Management and querying of many types of biological data	Genome Databases (eu), Algorithms and Analysis, EBI	BioMart
	BioSystems	Database of Biological Systems	Pathways, NCBI	NCBI BioSystems

	BLAST	Basic Local Alignment and Search Tool	Algorithms and Analysis, NCBI	NCBI BLAST

	Name	Description	Category	Resources
	CGAP	Characterize the molecular genetic changes that cause a normal cell to become a cancer cell	Variation & Medical	CGAP
	CleanEx	A Database of Heterogeneous Gene Expression Data Based on A Consistent Gene Nomenclature	Expression	CleanEx
	ClustalW2	Performs multiple sequence alignments	Algorithms and Analysis, EBI	Clustal W
	CMR	Comprehensive Microbial Resource	Genome Databases (pro), Nucleotides	TIGR Comprehensive Microbial Resource
	Complete Microbial Genomes	An extensive collection of data, resources and tools for prokaryotic genomic analysis	Genome Databases (pro), NCBI	Complete Microbial Genomes
	Complete Microbial Genomes	An extensive collection of data, resources and tools for prokaryotic genomic analysis	Genome Databases (pro), NCBI	Complete Microbial Genomes
	Consensus	A pattern and motif recognition program	Nucleotides, Proteins, Algorithms and Analysis	Consensus

Name	Description	Category	Resources

Controlled Vocabularies	Standardized term lists that can enhance interactions with biological databases	Literature and Text Mining	Controlled Vocabularies (including Open Biomedical Ontologies)
Cytoscape	An open-source software platform used for visualization and analysis of molecular interaction and network data	Pathways	Cytoscape
DAVID	A tool that analyzes large lists of genes to provide biological meaning	Expression, Pathways	DAVID
dbGaP	A database of genotypes and phenotypes with extensive variation data and clinical details	Variation & Medical, NCBI	dbGaP
dbSNP	NCBI's SNP database	Variation & Medical, NCBI	NCBI dbSNP
DBTSS	Database of Transcriptional Start Sites	Expression, Nucleotides	DBTSS
DCODE	DCODE.org Comparative Genomics Developments, a collection of powerful comparative genomics tools	Algorithms and Analysis, NCBI	Dcode.org anthology of comparative genomic tools

Name	Description	Category	Resources
DGV: Database of Genomic Variants	Database of Genomic Variants, DGV, catalogs and displays structural variation in the human genome	Variation & Medical	DGV: Database of Genomic Variants
DrugBank	A chemo informatics and bioinformatics resource	Genome Databases	Drug Bank

Name	Description	Category	Resources
		(eu)	
ENCODE Data at UCSC	ENCODE Data at UCSC	Genome Databases (eu)	ENCODE Data Coordination Center at UCSC
ENCODE Foundations	Encyclopedia of DNA Elements	Genome Databases (eu)	ENCODE Data Coordination Center at UCSC
Ensembl	Ensembl Genome Browser	Genome Databases (eu), EBI	Ensembl
Ensembl Legacy	Older version of Ensembl Genome Browser	Genome Databases (eu), Genome Databases (pro), EBI	Ensembl
Entrez Gene	NCBI's Entrez tool for gene-centric information	Nucleotides, NCBI	NCBI Entrez Gene
Entrez Overview	Overview of NCBI's Entrez Search Resource	Miscellaneous, NCBI	NCBI Entrez

Name	Description	Category	Resources
Entrez Protein	NCBI's Entrez Protein for amino acid-centric information	Proteins, NCBI	NCBI Protein database
FASTA	FASTA sequence algorithm	Algorithms and Analysis, EBI	FASTA
FlyBase	A resource for the genes, genome and molecular biology of Drosophila melanogaster and related species.	Genome Databases (eu)	FlyBase
Functional Glycomics Gateway	The home for Functional Glycomics research	Expression, Proteins	Consortium for Functional

Name	Description	Category	Resources
			Glycomics
GAD: Genetic Association Database	An archived database associating human genes and polymorphisms with diseases	Variation & Medical	GAD: Genetic Association Database
Galaxy	Analysis tools for researchers	Algorithms and Analysis	Galaxy
GBrowse	GBrowse User Introductory Tutorial	Genome Databases (eu), Genome Databases (pro)	GBrowse
Gene Expression Omnibus (GEO)	A gene expression / molecular abundance repository and a curetted, online resource for gene expression data	Expression, Algorithms and Analysis, NCBI	Gene Expression Omnibus (GEO)

Name	Description	Category	Resources
GeneMANIA	GeneMANIA: Fast Gene Function Predictions	Proteins, Pathways	GeneMANIA
Gene Ontology	Gene Ontology controlled vocabularies in biology	Literature and Text Mining	Gene Ontology (GO)
GeneSNPs	An integrated view of gene structure and SNP variations	Ye Olde Tutorials	GeneSNPs
GeneTests	GeneTests, a current, comprehensive genetic testing resource	Ye Olde Tutorials	GeneTests
Genetics Home Reference	A collection of data describing the effects of genetic variability on human health and disease	Variation & Medical	Genetics Home Reference
GenMAPP	A freely available open source software application for visualizing microarray data in the context of biological	Pathways	GenMAPP-- Gene Microarray Pathway Profiler

		pathways.		
	GenoCAD	Computer-Assisted Design software for synthetic biology	Nucleotides	GenoCAD
	GenoCAD Advanced Topics	Computer-Assisted Design software for synthetic biology	Nucleotides	GenoCAD

	Name	Description	Category	Resources
	Genome Variation Server (GVS)	A database providing rapid access to human genotype data and analysis tools.	Variation & Medical	GVS
	GENSAT	Provides an extensive amount of high quality images of gene expression in the central nervous system of the mouse.	Expression, NCBI	GENSAT
	Gibbs Motif Sampler	A motif finder and analysis tool	Nucleotides, Proteins, Algorithms and Analysis	Gibbs
	GoMiner	Ascribe biological significance to large lists of genes by annotating them with their corresponding GO categories	Algorithms and Analysis	GoMiner
	Gramene	A resource on rice and other grass genomes	Genome Databases (eu)	Gramene
	HapMap	HapMap, a database and analysis resource of human variation	Variation & Medical	HapMap
	iHOP	Information Hyperlinked Over Proteins text mining resource	Literature and Text Mining	iHOP
	IntAct protein interaction	IntAct is an open source database and analysis resource for protein	Proteins, Pathways,	IntAct

database	interaction data	EBI	

Name	Description	Category	Resources
Integrated Microbial Genomes (IMG)	IMG is a powerful community resource for the comparative analysis and annotation of microbial genome data.	Genome Databases (pro)	IMG
Integrated Microbial Genomes with Microbiome samples (IMG/M)	IMG/M provides tools for analyzing the functional capability of microbial communities based on their meta genome sequence	Genome Databases (pro)	IMG/M
InterPro	A comprehensive protein signature resource	Proteins, Algorithms and Analysis, EBI	The InterPro Database
KEGG	KEGG, The Kyoto Encyclopedia of Genes and Genomes	Pathways	KEGG
Madeline 2.0	Human pedigree diagram tools	Variation & Medical	Madeline 2.0
Map Viewer	Map Viewer Genome Browser from NCBI	Genome Databases (eu), NCBI	NCBI Map Viewer
MDscan	Motif Discovery scan for nucleotide and protein motifs	Nucleotides, Proteins, Algorithms and Analysis	MDscan
Melina II	A Web-Based Tool for Promoter Analysis	Nucleotides, Algorithms and Analysis	Melina II

Name	Description	Category	Resources

MEME Algorithm	Multiple Expectation Maximum for Motif Elicitation	Nucleotides, Proteins, Algorithms and Analysis	MEME
MEME Suite GLAM2 Algorithm	Part of a motif discovery tool that can detect conserved motifs in a set of DNA or protein sequences.	Algorithms and Analysis	GLAM2
MEME Suite Overview	Motif-based sequence analysis tools	Algorithms and Analysis	MEME
MEME Suite Sequence Annotation Tools	MEME suite motif finding and annotating tools	Algorithms and Analysis	MEME
MEME Suite TOMTOM and GOMO algorithms	Motif discovery tool that can detect conserved motifs in a set of DNA or protein sequences that you provide	Algorithms and Analysis	MEME
MINT	Molecular Interaction Database	Proteins, Pathways	MINT
miRBase	microRNA sequences, targets and gene nomenclature	Nucleotides	miRBase
MMDB	Molecular Modeling Database at NCBI	Proteins, NCBI	MMDB

Name	Description	Category	Resources
Mouse Genome Informatics (MGI)	The Mouse Genome Informatics resource provides data, tools, and analyses for the mouse model organism.	Genome Databases (eu)	Mouse Genome Informatics (MGI)

NCBI Overview	Home to many commonly used publicly available databases and tools in molecular biology.	Miscellaneous, NCBI	Database resources of the National Center for Biotechnology Information
NIEHS SNPs	National Institute for Environmental Health Sciences Environmental Genome Project (EGP) SNPs	Variation & Medical	NIEHS SNPs Program
OMIM	Online Mendelian Inheritance in Man (OMIM): A database of human genes, genetic diseases and disorders	Variation & Medical	OMIM
Overview of Genome Browsers	Various Genome Browsers examined	Genome Databases (eu), Genome Databases (pro)	GBrowse IMG Ensembl NCBI Map Viewer
Pathway Interaction Database	A resource of pathway and network data and displays	Proteins, Pathways	NCI / Nature Pathway Interaction Database

Name	Description	Category	Resources
Pfam	Protein Domain families	Proteins	Pfam
PhenomicDB	Phenotypes database	Expression, Variation & Medical	PhenomicDB
PlantGDB	Plant Genome Database	Genome Databases (eu)	PlantGDB
Primer3	Pick primers from a DNA sequence.	Nucleotides, Algorithms and Analysis	Primer3

PROSITE	Database of protein domains, families and functional sites	Proteins	PROSITE
PubMatrix	PubMatrix, an on-line tool for multiplex literature mining of the PubMed database.	Literature and Text Mining	PubMatrix
PubMed	PubMed access to biomedical research literature	Literature and Text Mining, Variation & Medical, NCBI	NCBI PubMed
Rat Genome Database (RGD)	Rat Genome Database	Genome Databases (eu)	Rat Genome Database (RGD)
RCSB PDB	RCSB Protein Data Bank	Proteins	RCSB PDB
Reactome	Knowledgebase of biological processes	Pathways	Reactome

Name	Description	Category	Resources
Reactome Legacy	Older version of the current Reactome knowledgebase of biological processes.	Pathways	Reactome
RefSeq	Provides molecular sequence records to help locate gene and protein data.	Nucleotides, NCBI	RefSeq
Saccharomyces Genome Database (SGD)	Saccharomyces Genome Database	Genome Databases (eu)	SGD
SeattleSNPs	Human SNPs in genes	Variation & Medical	SeattleSNPs
SMART	Protein domain annotation and analysis of domain architectures	Proteins	SMART

	STRING	known and predicted protein-protein interactions	Literature and Text Mining, Proteins, Pathways	STRING
	Structural Biology Knowledge base	The Protein Structure Initiative Structural Biology Knowledgebase	Proteins	The Protein Structure Initiative Structural Biology Knowledgebase
	TAIR	The Arabidopsis Information Resource	Genome Databases (eu)	The Arabidopsis Information Resource (TAIR)

	Name	Description	Category	Resources
	Textpresso	Text-mining the biological literature	Literature and Text Mining	Textpresso
	UCSC Archaeal Genome Browser	Provides you with many research and analysis tools that can be used to examine the genomes of more than 50 microbial species from the domain archaea.	Genome Databases (pro)	The UCSC Archaeal Genome Browser
	UCSC Genome Browser: An Introduction	The UCSC Genome Browser Introduction	Genome Databases (eu), Algorithms and Analysis	UCSC Genome Browser
	UCSC Genome Browser: Custom Tracks and Table Browser	UCSC Genome Browser advanced topics	Genome Databases (eu), Algorithms and Analysis	UCSC Genome Browser
	UCSC Genome Browser: The Additional Tools	Additional tools at the UCSC Genome Browser	Algorithms and Analysis, Expression, Genome Databases (eu), Nucleotides,	UCSC Genome Browser

		Proteins	
UniProt	UniProt, Universal Protein Resource	Proteins, Algorithms and Analysis	UniProt

Name	Description	Category	Resources
VBRC	The Viral Bioinformatics Resource Center	Genome Databases (pro), Algorithms and Analysis	VBRC
Viral Genomes at NCBI	Viral genome resources including single-stranded or double-stranded RNA or DNA viruses	Genome Databases (pro), NCBI	NCBI Viral Resources
VisANT	A web-based or downloadable software platform used for visualization and analysis of networks and interaction pathways	Pathways	VisANT
VISTA	Tools for Comparative Genomics	Algorithms and Analysis, Expression, Nucleotides, Variation & Medical	VISTA
World Tour of Genomics Resources	A World Tour of Genome Resources for finding and learning the right resource for your needs.	Algorithms and Analysis, Expression, Genome Databases (eu), Genome Databases (pro), Literature and Text Mining, Miscellaneous, Nucleotides, Pathways, Proteins, Variation & Medical	UCSC Genome Browser

Name	Description	Category	Resources
WormBase	molecular and genetic information on Caenorhabditis elegans and related species	Genome Databases (eu)	WormBase
WormBase	molecular and genetic information on Caenorhabditis elegans and related species	Genome Databases (eu)	WormBase
XplorMed	eXploring Medline abstracts	Literature and Text Mining	XplorMed
ZFIN	The Zebra fish Information Network	Genome Databases (eu)	ZFIN

Chapter 3: BIOINFORMATICS, INTERNET AND LINKS

Internet facilitates linking to current programs and initiatives utilizing the Internet to form clearing-houses and distributed networks of biological information. Some are integrated system for agricultural genome analysis, including databases, conferences, publications, courses, and a particularly good plant genome online database tutorial. Links to many tools and programs are available from the National Institutes of Health for sequence analysis and molecular biology, including databases, protocols and tutorials. Many a pages include links to a number of model organism databases, banks and tables, and to a number of genetic databases, Department of Molecular and Cellular Biology.

Searching: Various ways are available to search; a text-based query can be submitted through the system like Entrez system. A sequence query can be submitted through the program. To search a particular type of database or item, it should be selected from the menu. Various lists include a number of databases. The list can be accessed by category/type of database or alphabetically by title. By clicking on the short description of each database, a paragraph-long description can be accessed from the database. Another system, Sequence Retrieval System interface provides links to sites that allow web based searching and retrieval of nucleotide and protein sequence. With the **facility** to query most of the major **Bioinformatics** databases and retrieve textual information but it is not the complete list.

Like other fields of knowledge, **Bioinformatics** has grown and seeing the researches going on in the genetic scenario, nobody can ignore the increasing impact of **Bioinformatics**. We can relate it with the increasing impact of Internet in information scenario. The future holds the ever increasing dependability on information and information technology so it can be said that Internet is an efficient tool for accessing the Bio-information in the form of **Bioinformatics**. The need is to know, explore and exploiting it.

1. (www.cats.ucsc.edu)

2. (www.cato.com/biotech/)

3. (www.the-scientist.com)

4. (www.nbif.org/links/1.20.php)

5. (www.genomics.phrma.org/today/)

6. (www.gnn.tigr.org/main.shtml)

7. (www.ebi.ac.uk/ismb-97/papers2.html)

8. (www.cgl.ucsf.edu/psb/)

9. (www.Biosis.org.zrdocs/zoolinfo/biol_inf.htm)

10. (www.ars-genome.cornell.edu/)

11. (www.molbio.info.nih.gov/molbio/)

12. (www.golgi.harvard.edu/Biolinks.html)

13. (www.molbio.info.nih.gov/cgi-bin/pdb)

14. (www.oup.co.uk/bioinformatics/contents/)

15. (www.cgb.indiana.edu/bioinformatics/resources)

16. (www.genome.ucsc.edu/)

17. (www.ebi.ac.uk/index.html)

18. (www.atcc.org)

19. (www.bio.org/welcome.html)

20. (www.biotech-register.com/)

21. (www.nbif.org)

22. (www.proteome.com/services/index.html)

23. (www.rcsb.org/pdb/)

24. (www.sciewb.com)

25. (www.bioinfo.com/fbdhome.html)

26. (www.bioinformatics.org)

27. (www.yahoo.com)

28. (www.cbt.org)

29. (www.unipune.ernet.in)

30. (www.mcrcr0.med.nyu.edu/rcr/molbio/syllabus-98.html)

31. (www.ncbi.nlm.nih.gov/Entrez/index.html)

32. (www.ncbi.lm.nih.gov/BLAST)

Internet educational resources for Bioinformatics

NCBI: sequence data repository, US **Bioinformatics** center. (http://www.ncbi.nlm.nih.gov/)

EBI: sequence data repository, European **Bioinformatics** center. (http://www.ebi.ac.uk/)

Pasteur: France bioinfo. center, Bio Netbook is an excellent database of Internet information for biosciences, **Bioinformatics**. (http://bioweb.pasteur.fr/intro-uk.html) Bio Netbook

ExPASy/SWISSPROT: protein sequence data center. (http://www.expasy.ch/) good list of bioinfo resources

Sanger: European sequencing, **Bioinformatics** center. (http://www.sanger.ac.uk/)

Weizmann: Israel **Bioinformatics** center. (http://bioinformatics.weizmann.ac.il/)

GenomeWeb: **Bioinformatics** resources. (http://www.hgmp.mrc.ac.uk/GenomeWeb/)

CSHL: US sequencing, **Bioinformatics** center. (http://www.cshl.org/)

WUSTL: US sequencing, **Bioinformatics** center. (http://www.ibc.wustl.edu/)

Stanford genome center US sequencing, **Bioinformatics** center. (http://genome-www.stanford.edu/)

TIGR: US sequencing, **Bioinformatics** center. (http://www.tigr.org/)

Celera: US commercial sequencing, **Bioinformatics** center. (http://www.celera.com/)

GenomeNet : Japan **Bioinformatics** center (http://www.genome.ad.jp/)

Bionet: Usenet network news for biology. (http://www.bio.net/)

BioMedNet: **Bioinformatics** resources including HMS Beagle, (http://www.bmn.com/)

BioInform mostly commercial news, services - good list of companies in **Bioinformatics**. (http://www.bioinform.com/)

Web Sites in the News

a) *Bioinformatics via D'Trends*: A good place to begin your research on the field, because it provides all of the background information by the person who coined the term himself --Dr. Hwa A. Lim (aka HAL)

b) *Human Genome Project Information Web Site:* A government source and a great place to go for most of the information relating to current genome research. Sponsored by the U.S. Department of Energy Human Genome Program.

c) *The National Human Genome Research Institute (NHGRI):* Grant information, intramural research, ethical, legal and social implications, genomic and genetic resources. Also includes links to the policy and public affairs, workshops and conferences, and "The Genome Hub."

Bioinformatics homepage: Internet Resources for **Bioinformatics** Coordinator: Dr. George Michaels. The aim of this page is to provide CSI students and researchers of **Bioinformatics** and Computational Biology an internet resource for their research as well as news, events, activities.

NCBI: Bioinformatics Resources for Biosciences Researchers

What is NCBI? NCBI is the National Center for Biotechnology Information. The Center was founded in 1988 as a division of the National Library of Medicine (NLM) at the National Institutes of Health (NIH). The NCBI website contains several free computerized information-processing methods of biological information.

NCBI not only conducts research on biomedical problems at the molecular level using mathematical and computational methods, but also provides numerous free databases and molecular search tools, with extensive support documentation for these resources.

Why Use NCBI?

1) The Entrez search of NCBI allows a search across all databases: Genome, Gene, Protein, Nucleotide, even PubMed

2) NCBI gives you real-time results for all searches

3) NCBI's multi-database management allows you to go from one database to another without having to re-enter your search terms

Using This Guide: This guide is the same as the handout used in the Introduction to NCBI's Bioinformatics Resources class (http://www.galter.northwestern.edu/) offered by Galter Library. The class is only offered twice a year, but you can always schedule a session by request, or use this online guide to learn at your own pace.

If you would like to follow the steps and examples described in this guide, it is recommended that you **open the NCBI website in another browser window** and re-size the browser windows so both the guide and the NCBI pages can be viewed simultaneously.

Currently there is one video tutorial contained in this guide, located in the MapViewer section (http://www.galter.northwestern.edu/ guides-and-tutorials/ncbi-bioinformatics-resources-for-biosciences-researchers#MapViewerwithVideoTutorial). More videos are being developed and will be added to this guide as they are created.

Accessing NCBI's Cross-Database Search Page

Go to (http://www.ncbi.nlm.nih.gov/)

Navigation Hints: There are shortcuts and menus on all NCBI database pages:

1)   Top-of-page menu bar shortcuts will take you to other major NCBI tools

2)   Right-side pull-down menus for each entry will take you to related records

3)   To get back to the NCBI home page at any time, just click the NCBI logo in the upper left of any screen

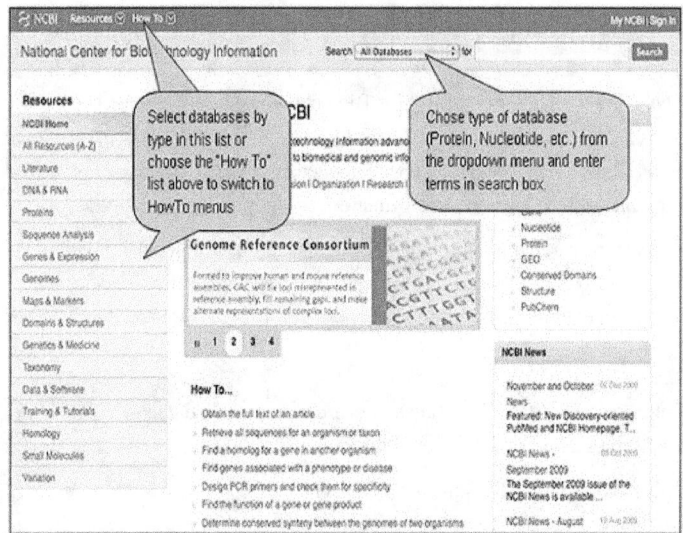

Start with a General Search: Search terms can be entered just as in PubMed:

1)   You can use Boolean terms (AND, OR)

2)   You can supply qualifiers in square brackets [au] = author, [organism], etc.

Try a search for "tubby" (a gene for obesity in mice with homologues in humans, rats, and other species) and "homo sapiens" as organism:

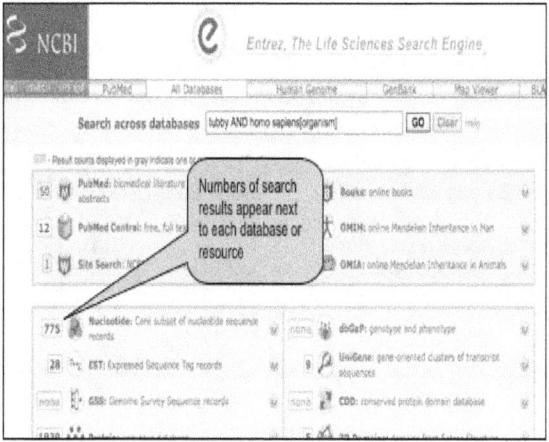

GenBank: NCBI's Genetic Information Repository and Entrez Nucleotide Database

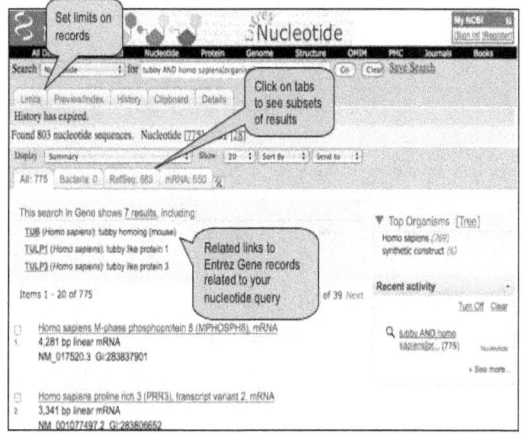

On this screen

1) **Display** allows you to view records as FASTA, GenBank or other styles
2) **Mark** a record by clicking the **checkbox** beside an entry
3) Set **limits** for a more defined search
4) View the full record for any entry by clicking its Name/title

None of the records on this first page appear to be tubby itself, but Entrez helpfully suggests links in the Entrez Gene database that may be related to your search, so **click on the link to the Entrez Gene record for "TUB" in the Gene results box at the top of the page**.

Entrez Gene

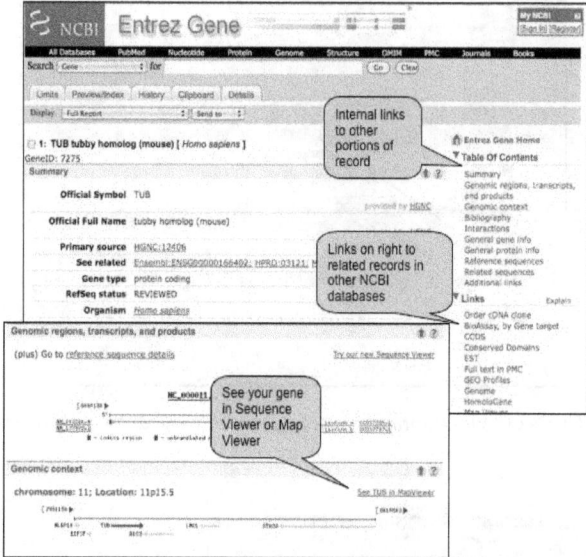

On this screen

1) **Link** to related records in other NCBI databases through menu on right
2) Jump to **Map Viewer** or **Sequence Viewer**
3) Read **GeneRIF**s (references from the literature supporting the genes function)
4) **View** transcript regions and protein products
5) See where the gene lies on the chromosome and its nearest neighbours
6) View information from other databases such as Gene Ontology
7) For more detail on the gene, its location on the chromosome and homologous genes in other species, go to Map Viewer
8) **Click** "See TUB in Map Viewer"

MapViewer (with Video Tutorial)

On this 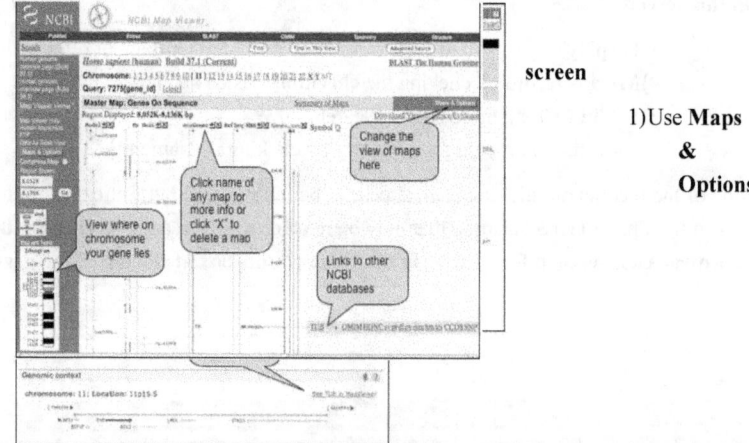 screen

1) Use **Maps** & **Options**

button to view the genomic maps of other species in this region for interspecies homology or to add specific types of maps to view (CpG islands, etc.)

2) View contigs, coding sequences
3) View neighboring genes
4) **Zoom** in or zoom out
5) **BLAST** the human genome using the direct link to genomic BLAST
6) **Link** to other databases, such as OMIM, through the links in pinkish menu bar
7) **Click** on the **SNP** link in the pinkish label box

Entrez SNP

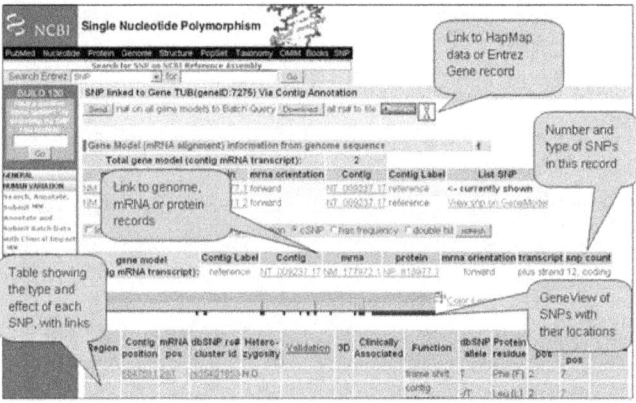

On this screen

1) View **location** and **type** of SNPs on a gene model, and **link** to each record in the Entrez SNP database
2) **Link** to HapMap data for variation in your gene or to Entrez Gene record
3) **Link** to records for genome contig, mRNA and protein records for your gene
4) View types of validation models for SNPs
5) **Click on the mRNA link** in the gene model box **(NM_177972)**

Entrez Nucleotide

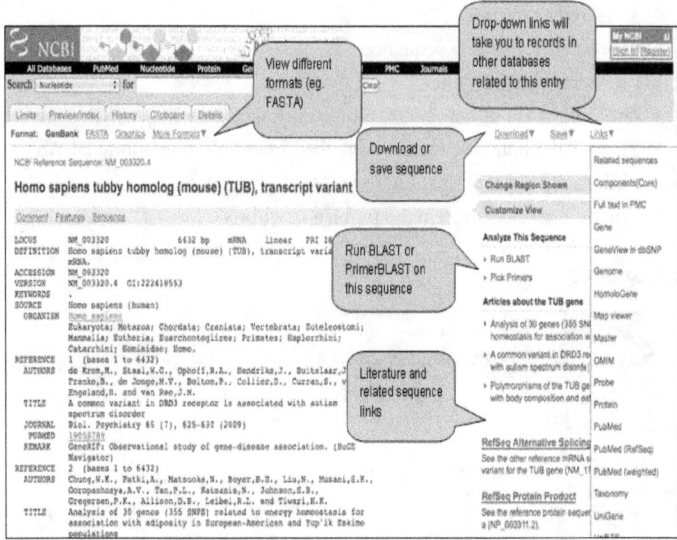

On this screen

1) **Links** pull-down menu to right allows you to link to related records for this entry in other NCBI databases

2) **Click Protein**

Entrez Protein

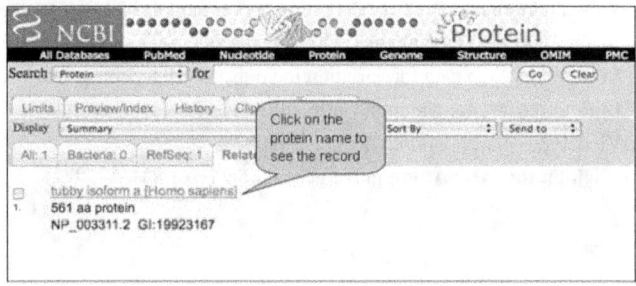

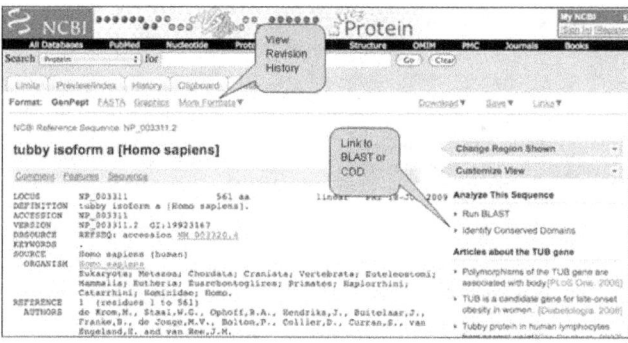

On this screen

    a. Set **Limits**, change the **Display**

    b. Through the drop-down **Links** menu:

        i. Do a quick **BLink** (BLAST Link) to get an automatic BLAST of similar proteins

        ii. Check the protein for **Conserved Domains**

    c. Check the sequence **Revision History** (More Formats drop-down menu)

    d. **Click BLink** (from the pull-down Links menu)

Viewing Related Sequences and Structures: Performing a BLAST through the BLAST interface requires you to enter the sequence as FASTA format. Clicking the **BLink link** from any protein record will take you to a **page of pre-run BLAST sequence similarities**.

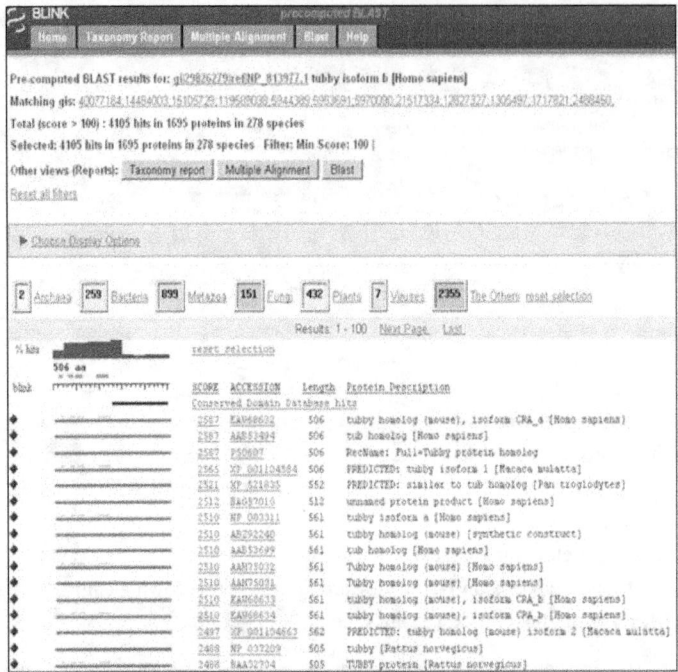

The MMDB and Viewing Structures with Cn3D: From your Protein view page, **check the links on the right** for a **Structure** or **Related Structure** link. If there are no solved structures or related structures for your protein, you won't see any structure links.

Alternatively, you can **go back to the NCBI home page** at (http://www.ncbi.nlm.nih.gov/) and search for your protein structure by setting the pull-down menu to **Structure** and typing your query protein in the search box (e.g., tubby). This will give you a list of possible crystal structures for your protein. Select one by clicking on the Accession Number. This will take you to the **MMDB (Molecular Modeling Database)** structure page.

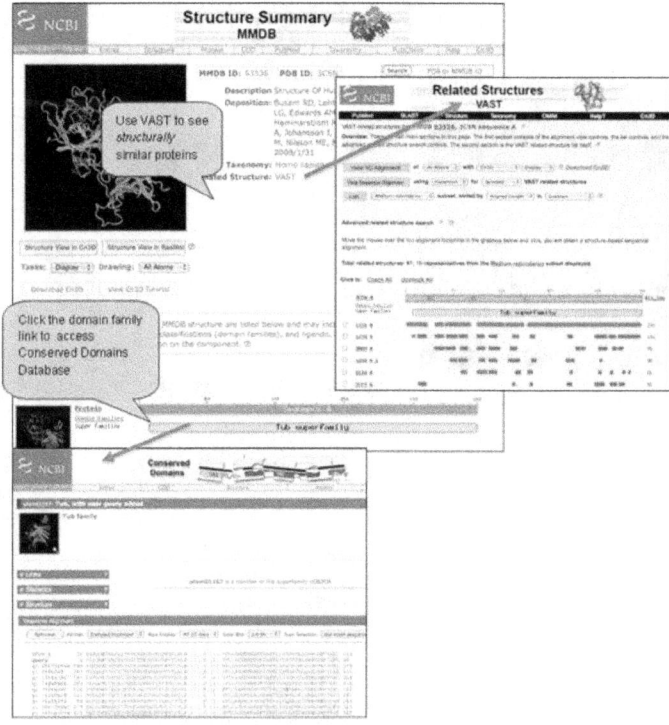

On the Structure Summary screen

1) View the **crystal structure** of the protein

2) Run a **structure similarity search (VAST)** which finds other proteins with similar 3D structures (different from BLAST, which finds sequence similarities) of any of the chains of the protein

3) View the **citation** in which the structure was first characterized

In order to view structures, you ***must*** install the Cn3D software on your computer. It is a free download from NCBI. You can access the download page from http://www.ncbi.nlm.nih.gov/Structure/CN3D/ cn3d.shtml and follow the installation instructions.

Once you have Cn3D installed, you can open and view the crystal structure for your protein by clicking on the button **View 3D Structure** on any structure page. This will open a pop-up window that asks you to choose the program to open the molecule, with Cn3D as the default. Click **OK**.

This will open the molecule in a new window, laid over your MMDB structure page:

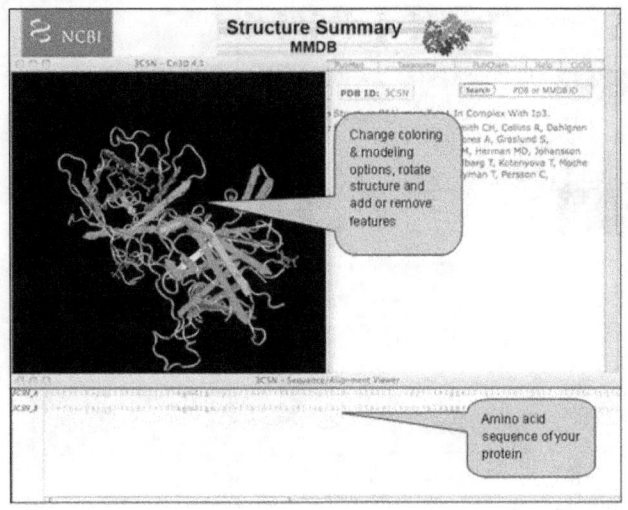

Other Useful Databases and Tools @ NCBI

1) OMIM – Online Mendelian Inheritance in Man
2) Amino Acid Explorer
3) PubChem (chemical database)
4) NCBI Bookshelf (free online texts)
5)   Genome Workbench (download the desktop application)   and lots more
...

Source: (http://www.galter.northwestern.edu/signin)

NCBI   Educational   Resources: The   NCBI   Education   Page
(http://www.galter.northwestern.edu/signin) includes links to all sorts of NCBI tutorials and
materials including -

NCBI Handbook
BLAST Tutorial
BLAST Guide
Cn3D Structure tutorial
NCBI's Science Primer

Further Help

For assistance in using any of the NCBI tools and databases, email or call (312-503-
8689) Pamela   Shaw,   Biosciences   &   Bioinformatics   Librarian
(http://www.galter.northwestern.edu/contact/ Galter/Reference).

General Molecular Biology Websites: Sites that link to other sites

Online Tools @ http://molbiol-tools.ca/ - Has links to molecular biology pages all over the place.

More organized collections of Web resources

BCM Search Launcher (http://searchlauncher.bcm.tmc.edu/) - The Baylor College of Medicine Search Launcher is an on-going project to organize molecular biology-related search and analysis services available on the WWW by function by providing a single point-of-entry for related searches.

SeWeR @ http://www.bioinformatics.org/sewer/ - Sequence analysis using Web Resources. A unified interface for diverse web resources.

JustBio.com @ http://www.justbio.com/ - Contains some hosted tools not present on the other mega-sites.

Bioinformatics Servers

EBI Tools @ http://www.ebi.ac.uk/services - Blast, Fasta, Sequence Analysis, Homology Searches, Sequence Translation, Protein Annotation, Genomes, Proteomes, Sequence Alignments, **including Clustal** @ http://www.ebi.ac.uk/Tools/msa/

Expasy @ http://www.expasy.org/ - Proteomics server at Swiss Institute of Bioinformatics.

NCBI genomics Tools @ http://www.ncbi.nlm.nih.gov/ guide/all/#tools_ - NCBI's tools for genomics

Fly Stuff

BDGP Analysis Tools page @ http://www.fruitfly.org/ seq_tools/other.html - Search the *Drosophila* genome, predict genes etc.

Top @ http://fruitfly4.aecom.yu.edu/molbio.html#top

EMBOSS (The European Molecular Biology Open Software Suite):

EMBOSS homepage @ http://emboss.sourceforge.net/ - Description of the EMBOSS suite.

EMBOSS Applications - ...at the EMBNET node in Madrid.

EMBOSS Software via the WWW - ...at University of Victoria.

Primer Design: Primer 3 at Whitehead Institute - PCR primer selection tool.

dCAPS Finder 2.0 @ http://helix.wustl.edu/dcaps/dcaps.html - Web-based primer design for single nucleotide polymorphism analysis.

Tandem Repeat Finders - Useful tool for finding potential STR polymorphisms:

Tandem Repeats Finder @ http://tandem.bu.edu/trf/trf.submit.options.html - "A tandem repeat in DNA is two or more adjacent, approximate copies of a pattern of nucleotides. Tandem Repeats Finder is a program to locate and display tandem repeats in DNA sequences."

Simple Sequence Repeats (SSR) Extractor Utility @ http://www.aridolan.com/ssr/ssr.aspx - The SSR Extractor utility finds simple sequence repeats within DNA sequences (loaded from any local Fasta file) and displays them in a table. The input data is processed according to several user-defined parameters. The output table is interactive and supports filtering, sorting, data re-processing and exporting to CSV format (Excel).

DHPLC Stuff

DHPLC tools @ **Stanford** (http://insertion.stanford.edu/ dhplc.html) - Useful things for designing ample icons for the WAVE machine

Transgenomic @ http://www.transgenomic.com/ - Transgenomic's home page.

Other stuff - Things to help with cloning and the like:

CloneIt! - A program for finding sub-cloning strategies, in-frame deletions and frame shifts using restriction enzymes and DNA polymerases.

Webcutter @ http://www.firstmarket.com/cutter/cut2.html - Webcutter.

Resources at Einstein - Servers:

Seqweb @ **Harryeagle** - seqweb on Harryeagle.aecom.yu.edu . No longer working - that's why I made this list.

Sequence Analysis @ **AECOM** - seqweb and GCG services at Einstein.

Lab web pages with useful links: **Morrow** (http://www.einstein.yu.edu/error-pages/404.aspx?aspxerrorpath=/morrow/#C) | **Greally** |

Sequence Analysis Tools

Other Analytical Tools

1) HOME (http://phobos.ramapo.edu/~pbagga/index.html)
2) Comparison & Alignments (http://phobos.ramapo.edu/ ~pbagga/binf/binf_res/ bioinfo_sat_comp.htm)
3) Functional Analysis (http://phobos.ramapo.edu/~pbagga/ binf/binf_res/bioinfo_sat_func.htm)
4) Structural Analysis (http://phobos.ramapo.edu/ ~pbagga/binf/binf_res/ bioinfo_sat_struc.htm)

5) Other Analytical Tools (http://phobos.ramapo.edu/ ~pbagga/binf/binf_res/ bioinfo_sat_other.htm)

ACEDB : A. C. Elegans Data Base (http://www.sanger.ac.uk/ resources/software/) - A software tool to manage and provide easy access to large collections of genomic data.

BCM Search Launcher (http://searchlauncher.bcm.tmc.edu/) - An on-going project to organize molecular biology-related search and analysis services available on the WWW by function by providing a single point-of-entry for related searches.

BCM ReadSeq (http://dot.imgen.bcm.tmc.edu:9331/seq-util/ redseq.html) - Allows converting Sequence Formats using ReadSeq method.

BIMAS: Bioinformatics & Molecular Analysis Section (http://bimas.dcrt.nih.gov/) - The BIMAS provides guidance, support and resources to scientists throughout the NIH in the genomic and genetic analysis fields of Bioinformatics.

BIOLOGY WORKBENCH (http://workbench.sdsc.edu/) - Database searching integrated with access to a wide variety of analysis and modeling tools, all within a point and click interface that eliminates file format compatibility problems.

Biotoolkit (http://www.biosupplynet.com/btk08/) - Hundreds of advanced online tools for molecular biology data retrieval, analysis, and visualization. Also provides annotated links to web tools for the study of nucleic acid, genome, and protein structure.

CBRG: Computational Biochemistry Research Group (http://www.cbrg.ethz.ch/) - This server offers many free and helpful services and tools for Computational Biologists, Biochemists, and Molecular Evolutionists.

CBS distanceP (http://www.cbs.dtu.dk/services/distanceP/): The server predicts distance constraints between amino acids in proteins from the amino acid sequence.

Comparative Sequence Analysis (http://www.bork.embl-heidelberg.de/Frame/) - Here you can test your DNA sequence for sequencing errors.

CUBIC (http://cubic.bioc.columbia.edu/) - Columbia University Bioinformatics center services PredictProtein, META, PredictNLS, and EVA.

DARWIN: Data Analysis and Retrieval with Indexed Nucleotide/Peptide Sequences (http://cbrg.inf.ethz.ch/subsection3_1_7. html) - An interactive tool for peptide and nucleotide sequence analysis. A growing library of functions for sequence management and analysis, statistics, numeric, graphics, parallel execution and more.

DAS: Transmembrane Prediction Server (http://www.sbc.su.se/ ~miklos/DAS/) - Predicts transmembrane regions of a query sequence. A number of algorithms designed to identify putative transmembrane helices in the primary amino acid sequence have been developed, and current methods can identify around 90-95% of all true transmembrane segments with an over-prediction rate of only a few percent.

Divide-and-Conquer Multiple Sequence Alignment (http://bibiserv.techfak.uni-bielefeld.de/dca/) - A program for producing fast, high quality simultaneous multiple sequence alignments of amino acid, RNA, or DNA sequences.

DNA Primer Melt Calculator (http://www.strauss.lanl.gov/outgoing/DNAprimer/DNAprimer.html) - A handy calculator of PCR primers for DNA Transformation in a nice justified layout of the sequence with cod on numbering.

DOGS: Database Of Genome Sizes (http://www.cbs.dtu.dk/ databases/DOGS/ index.php) - The purpose of this database is to provide a comprehensive list of estimated genome sizes for different organisms.

Dr. Tsong-Li Wang's Web Page (http://www.cis.njit.edu/~jason/) - A collection of sequence analysis tool.

Electronic PCR (http://www.ncbi.nlm.nih.gov/STS/) - PCR-based sequence tagged sites (STSs) have been used as landmarks for construction of various types of genomic maps. Using "electronic PCR" (e-PCR), these sites can be detected in DNA sequences, potentially allowing their map locations to be determined.

Embl Amino Acid Analysis Server (http://www.embl. heidelberg.de/aaa.html) - A server for protein and amino acid analysis.

EMBOSS (http://emboss.sourceforge.net/) - "The European Molecular Biology Open Software Suite". EMBOSS is a free Open Source software analysis package specially developed for the needs of the molecular biology (e.g. EMBnet) user community. The software automatically copes with data in a variety of formats and even allows transparent retrieval of sequence data from the web. Also, as extensive libraries are provided with the package, it is a platform to allow other scientists to develop and release software in true open source spirit. EMBOSS also integrates a range of currently available packages and tools for sequence analysis into a seamless whole. EMBOSS breaks the historical trend towards commercial software packages.

EMBOSS Sequence Analysis Servers (http://emboss.sourceforge.net/servers/) - A suite of free software tools for sequence analysis, including that of GCG. There are a wide variety of programs that make up the suite, ranging in application from database searching to presentation of sequence data.

ExPASy Proteomics Tools (http://www.expasy.org/tools/) - Provides tools from the ExPASy server as well as a few other servers.

ExPASy: Expert Protein Analysis System (http://www.expasy.org/) - This server is dedicated to the analysis of protein sequences and structures as well as 2-D PAGE.

ExPASy 3Dcrunch (http://swissmodel.expasy.org/) - The aim of 3Dcrunch is to submit all entries of the SWISS-PROT and trEMBL databases to SWISS-MODEL. Furthermore, all sequences of bacterial origin will be submitted to fold the recognition algorithm implemented in FoldFit. Taken together, these approaches will yield structural models for all sequences with clear similarities to proteins of know 3-D structure and a suggested fold class for all bacterial sequences.

FASTA Programs at the University of Virginia (http://alpha10.bioch.virginia. edu/fasta/) - This web page provides a table of FASTA programs at the University of Virginia.

Gcg: Genetics Computer Group (http://www.ggi.com/) - It enables scientists to analyze DNA and protein sequences by editing, mapping, comparing, and aligning them. Other programs facilitate RNA secondary structure prediction, DNA fragment assembly, and evolutionary analysis. GCG serves molecular biologists by building practical tools that implement the most important techniques of mathematical biology.

Genefisher (http://bibiserv.techfak.uni-bielefeld.de/genefisher2/) - An interactive PCR primer design program that will process aligned or unaligned sequences.

GENEMARK (http://genemark.biology.gatech.edu/GeneMark/index.html) - GeneMark, gene prediction algorithm, has been used for the analysis of EST sequences as well as for predicting rather long exons and designing RT-PCR primers.

Genetic Code Viewer (http://www.ebi.ac.uk/cgi-bin/mutations/ trtables.cgi) - Genetic Code Viewer is a simple tool for showing different versions of genetic code used by various taxonomic groups.

GenomeAtlas (http://www.cbs.dtu.dk/services/GenomeAtlas/) - The DNA Structural Atlas is a method of visualizing structural features within large regions of DNA. It was originally designed for analysis of complete genomes, but can also be used quite readily for analysis of regions of DNA as small as a few thousand bp in length.

Jambw: Java-based Molecular Biology Workbench (http://www.embl-heidelberg.de/~toldo/JaMBW.html) - The programs and documentation have been put together in order to try to give a free access to the exploitation of the most common bioinformatics operations that a molecular biologist currently has.

LabOnWeb (http://www.labonweb.com/) - Life science research engine. A collection of gene discovery tools designed to accelerate work in the lab, improve the quality and accuracy of experiments, simplify the delivery of information and help researchers make more informed decisions throughout the discovery process.

Large Dot Plots (http://alces.med.umn.edu/rawdot.html) - This page accesses a very fast dot plot algorithm designed for large DNA sequences.

MODELLER (http://guitar.rockfeller.edu/modeller/modeller.html) - MODELLER is most frequently used for homology or comparative modeling of protein three-dimensional structure: the user provides an alignment of a sequence to be modeled with known related structures and MODELLER will automatically calculate a full-atom model. More generally, MODELLER models protein 3D structure by satisfaction of spatial restraints.

Nps@: Network Protein Sequence Analysis (http://npsa-pbil.ibcp.fr/cgi-bin/npsa_automat.pl?page=/NPSA/npsa_server.html): An interactive web server dedicated to protein sequence analysis and available for the biologist community.

PATSCAN (http://www-unix.mcs.anl.gov/compbio/PatScan/ HTML/patscan.html) - A pattern matcher, which searches protein or nucleotide (DNA, RNA, tRNA etc.) sequence archives for instances of a pattern, which you input.

PCR Primer Selection (http://alces.med.umn.edu/rawprimer. html) - This page provides an interface to a PCR primer selection program based on xprimer.

PEDANT: Protein Extraction, Description, and Analysis Tool (http://pedant.mips.biochem.mpg.de/) - A software system for completely automatic and exhaustive analysis of protein sequence sets - from individual sequences to complete genomes.

Phylogeny Programs (http://evolution.genetics.washington.edu/ phylip/software.html): A comprehensive compilation of available phylogeny programs

Primer 3 (http://www.genome.wi.mit.edu/cgi-bin/primer/ primer3_www.cgi) - Designs PCR primers from a nucleotide sequence.

RasMol & Chime: Molecular Visualization Freeware (http://www.umass.edu/microbio/rasmol/) - RasMol is free software for looking at molecular structures. Chime shows molecules like RasMol, but unlike RasMol, Chime shows molecules inside a web page.

RDP: Ribosomal Database Project II (http://www.cme. msu.edu/RDP/html/ index.html) - Provides ribosome related data services, including online data analysis, rRNA derived phylogenetic trees, and aligned and annotated rRNA sequences.

ReadSeq (at BCM) (http://dot.imgen.bcm.tmc.edu:9331/seq-util/readseq.html) - Allows to convert Sequence Formats using ReadSeq method.

Repeat Finder (http://www.proweb.org/Tools/selfblast.html/) - Finds a repeat in a DNA of protein sequence using BLAST.

Repeatmasker Web Server (http://ftp.genome.washington.edu/ cgi-bin/RepeatMasker) - Repeatmasker screens DNA sequences in fasta format against a library of repetitive elements and returns a masked query sequence ready for database searches as well as a table annotating the masked regions.

RIFLE: Rapid Identification by Fragment Length Evaluation (http://bibiserv. techfak.uni-bielefeld.de/RIFLE/) - Compares restriction patterns of possibly unknown microorganisms against a database of theoretical restriction patterns generated from a 16S rDNA database. Restriction patterns of multiple restriction enzymes can be combined to improve the quality of identification; additional parameters allow the individual adaptation to laboratory processes.

RNA Movies (http://bibiserv.techfak.uni-bielefeld.de/rnamovies/) - A system for the visualization of RNA secondary structure spaces. Its input is a script consisting of primary and secondary structure information. From this script, the system generates animated graphical structure representations.

ROSE : Random-model of Sequence Evolution (http://bibiserv.techfak.uni-bielefeld.de/rose/) - Rose implements a new probabilistic model of the evolution of RNA, DNA, or protein-like sequences. The data created by *Rose* are suitable for the evaluation of methods in multiple sequence alignment computation and the prediction of phylogenetic relationships.

SBASE (http://www3.icgeb.trieste.it/~sbaserv/) - A protein domain library sequences that contains 237.937 annotated structural, functional, ligand-binding and topogenic segments of proteins, cross-referenced to all major sequence databases and sequence pattern collections.

SOM-BLOCK (http://www2.bioinf.mdc-berlin.de/block/ home7.html) - A method based on self-organizing maps (SOMs) to find patterns in protein sequences.

SRPDB: Signal Recognition Particle Database (http://psyche.uthct.edu/dbs/SRPDB/SRPDB.html) - Provides Aligned, Annotated and Phylogenetically Ordered Sequences Related to Structure and Function of SRP.

TESS: Transcription Element Search System (http://www.cbil.upcnn.edu/tess/): Searches a nucleic acid sequence for potential transcription factor binding sites from the Transfac database.

The Bio-Web Tools (http://cellbiol.com/Tools.html) - A comprehensive list of Sequence analysis tools.

The Gene Discovery Page (http://www3rdmill.com/ discovery.htm) - If your sequence analysis needs are basic, you are invited to use The Gene Discovery Page for your Bioinformatics solutions. The Gene Discovery Page organizes select web-accessible bioinformatics tools in a coherent fashion.

The Genome Channel (http://compbio.ornl.gov/channel/ index.html) - A tool for the comprehensive sequence-based view of genomes.

TRADAT: TRAnscription Databases and Analysis Tools) http://www.itba.mi.cnr.it/ tradat/) - Databases that collect experimental relevant data such as TRANSFAC and EPD provide the basis for sequence analysis.

Virtual Genome Center (http://alces.med.umn.edu/VGC.html) - This website provides several bioinformatics tools ranging from database searches to a variety of sequence analysis tools.

Webcutter (http://tools.neb.com/NEBcutter2/) - A tool by New England Biollabs (NEB) to help restriction map nucleotide sequences. In addition to restriction site mapping, Webcutter 2 also performs degenerate digests, including the option of finding restriction sites that can be introduced into a sequence by silent mutagenesis ("silent cutters").

Back to the Top	Bioinformatics Resources Home	Contact
(http://phobos.ramapo. edu/~pbagga/binf/ binf_res/bioinfo_ sat_other.htm#top)	(http://phobos.ramapo.edu/~pbagga/ binf/binf_res/binf_int_res.htm)	

HOME	Bioinf. Resources Home	Bioinformatics Center	DB Searching Tools
(http://phobos.ramapo. edu/~pbhaga/index. html)	(http://phobos.ramapo. edu/~pbhaga/binf/binf_ res/binf_int_res.htm)	(http://phobos.ramapo. edu/~pbhaga/binf/ binf_ res/binf_center.htm)	(http://phobos.ramapo. edu/~pbagga/binf/binf_ res/bioinfo_dbsearch. htm)
Genomic DBs	Taxonomic & Phylogenetic DBs	Sequence Retrieval	Sequence DBs
(http://phobos.ramapo. edu/~pbhaga/binf/ binf_res/bioinfo_ gndb_gen.htm)	(http://phobos.ramapo. edu/~pbhaga/binf/binf_ res/bioinfo_taxo.htm)	(http://phobos.ramapo. edu/~pbhaga/binf/binf_ res/bioinfo_seqret.htm)	(http://phobos.ramapo. edu/~pbagga/binf/binf_ res/bioinfo_seqdb_ na.htm)
Structural DBs	Specialized DBs	Seq. Analysis Tools	Software
(http://phobos.ramapo. edu/~pbhaga/binf/ binf_res/bioinfo_ struc_na.htm)	(http://phobos.ramapo. edu/~pbhaga/binf/binf_ res/bioinfo_specdb.htm)	(http://phobos.ramapo. edu/~pbhaga/binf/binf_ res/bioinfo_sat_ comp.htm)	(http://phobos.ramapo. edu/~pbagga/binf/binf_ res/bioinfo_soft.htm)
Biblio. Resources	Education/Research	Bioinformatics Servers	Misc. Resources
(http://phobos.ramapo. edu/~pbhaga/binf/ binf_res/bioinfo_ biblio_db.htm)	(http://phobos.ramapo. edu/~pbhaga/binf/binf_ res/bioinfo_edu_ edu.htm)	(http://phobos.ramapo. edu/~pbhaga/binf/binf_ res/bioinfo_serv.htm)	(http://phobos.ramapo. edu/~pbhaga/binf/binf_ res/bioinfo_misc.htm)

[Source: (http://www.ccg.unam.mx/~vinuesa/Bioinformatics_resources_web.html)]

Chapter 4: VIDEO TUTORIALS

Important Tutorial Videos

Bioinformatics Tutorials & Articles are here. Tutorials classified laying foundation course for both science and computer students for those aspiring bioinformatics. List also includes Bioinformatics Tutorials & Articles related to various tools.

(http://digitalworldbiology.com/dwb/bioinformatics-tutorials)

(http://www.youtube.com/watch?v=UohaqFb8_ME)

(http://nihlibrary.nih.gov/Services/Bioinformatics/Pages/Biotutorials.aspx)

(https://www.countway.harvard.edu/menuNavigation/libraryServices/classes/videoTutorials.html)

(http://www.youtube.com/user/bimaticsblog)

(http://bioinformaticsonline.com/bookmarks/view/3868/next-generation-sequencing-ngs-tutorials)

(http://mybio.wikia.com/wiki/Tutorials_in_bioinformatics)

(http://lectures.molgen.mpg.de/online_lectures.html)

(http://www.bioperl.org/wiki/HOWTO:Beginners#Abstract)

(http://www.ccg.unam.mx/~vinuesa/Bioinformatics_resources_web.html)

Video Tutorials

1) Imp: (http://digitalworldbiology.com/dwb/bioinformatics-tutorials)

2) (http://www.youtube.com/watch?v=UohaqFb8_ME)

3) (http://nihlibrary.nih.gov/Services/Bioinformatics/Pages/Biotutorials.aspx)

4) (https://www.countway.harvard.edu/menuNavigation/libraryServices/classes/videoTutorials.html)

5) (http://www.youtube.com/user/bimaticsblog)

6) (http://bioinformaticsonline.com/bookmarks/view/3868/next-generation-sequencing-ngs-tutorials

7) (http://mybio.wikia.com/wiki/Tutorials_in_bioinformatics)

8) (http://lectures.molgen.mpg.de/online_lectures.html)

9) (http://www.bioperl.org/wiki/HOWTO:Beginners#Abstract)

10) (http://www.ccg.unam.mx/~vinuesa/Bioinformatics_resources_web.html)

UTUBE VIDEOs

Tutorial videos of bioinformatics resources: online distribution trial in Japan named Togo TV

In recent years, biological web resources such as databases and tools have become more complex because of the enormous amounts of data generated in the field of life sciences. Traditional methods of distributing tutorials include publishing textbooks and posting web documents, but these static contents cannot adequately describe recent dynamic web services. Due to improvements in computer technology, it is now possible to create dynamic content such as video with minimal effort and low cost on most modern computers. The ease of creating and distributing video tutorials instead of static content improves accessibility for researchers, annotators and curators. This section focuses on online video repositories for educational and tutorial videos provided by resource developers and users. It also describes a project in Japan named Togo TV (http://togotv.dbcls.jp/en/) and discusses the production and distribution of high-quality tutorial videos, which would be useful to viewer, with examples. This article intends to stimulate and encourage researchers who develop and use databases and tools to distribute how-to videos as a tool to enhance product usability.

Recent advances in life sciences technology have dramatically changed the research style from hypothesis-driven research (bottom-up style) to data-driven research (top-down style). Current 'omics' projects have produced vast amounts of data that have been stored in various online databases. Simultaneously, many types of web tools have been developed to analyze the stored data. Traditional methods for distributing educational content include publishing textbooks and web documents. Although the contents of a textbook are sustainable, they quickly become obsolete because of frequent updates of web interfaces and improvement in web service functions.

Online Video Repositories

Several web services are already available for video distribution. YouTube is the most popular online video sharing service, and it contains many tutorial videos and lectures in many fields. Similarly, there are repository services such as Dailymotion and Vimeo (for more examples, see the Wikipedia article entitled 'List of video hosting services'). Most services are free to use, and any registered user can upload video. Live streaming services such as Ustream, Justin.tv and Stickam also exist. As the term 'live streaming' suggests, these services provide live streaming services for lectures, workshops, seminars and meetings that are recorded and may be played back at a later time.

In the scientific field, the *Journal of Visualized Experiments* has been published since 2006. It is a peer-reviewed, PubMed-indexed journal devoted to the publication of biological research in a video format. SciVee offers a comprehensive set of rich media solutions to enhance the discovery and collaboration of knowledge. It provides *Video and Podcasts* (standard videos and podcasts), *PubCast* (synchronized video abstracts of peer-reviewed articles), *PaperCast* (synchronized video abstracts of non-peer-reviewed articles), *SlideCast* (synchronized videos of slide presentations) and PosterCast (synchronized videos of posters or other conference presentations) in collaboration with scientists and researchers, as well as journals and publishers, societies, conference organizers, universities and research institutions. Dnatube is a community-based repository of scientific videos including educational materials, seminars and lectures. This site has over 5000 videos and 30 000 community members. Individual videos can be found using keyword search, category tags and topics.

Some universities and organizations also administer a video repository server, especially for providing lecture videos that are part of OpenCourseWare (OCW). The Massachusetts Institute of Technology (MIT) hosts MIT OCW and MIT World, and the University of Tokyo provides UT OCW. Academic Earth provides online courses of the world's top scholars from Harvard University and Stanford University among other top academic institutions. YouTube also has a special channel for education from colleges and universities named YouTube EDU, and another channel, Technology, Entertainment, Design (TED), delivers interesting lectures by respected individuals. A complete list of OCW websites is found at the OCW Consortium Website, and other useful services are listed in the Wikipedia article entitled 'List of educational video websites'.

In addition to repository-type services, delivery-type services named vodcasts (video podcasts) are available via Really Simple Syndication (RSS) technology. If a user subscribes to a podcast program in a vodcast player such as iTunes, the contents of the program are automatically updated when new content arrives. Since the vodcast programs can be transferred to portable devices such as the iPod, iPhone or iPad, the user can watch them anytime, anywhere. Although vodcast programs are mainly focused on news, entertainment and fashion, educational programs are also provided. Indeed, some institutes have already used the podcast/vodcast for education. Apple collects and webcasts educational contents via the iTunes store called iTunes U.

Video Tutorials Provided by Resource Developers and Users

As noted earlier, the publishing of tutorial videos by some providers has increased as the creation and distribution costs of videos have decreased. For example, National Center for Biotechnology Information provides tutorial videos of some services both on the YouTube channel and on their server such as dbGaP, the database of Genotypes and Phenotypes, that archives and distributes the results of studies that have investigated the interaction of genotype and phenotype and PubMed that is a database of citations and abstracts for biomedical literature from MEDLINE and additional life sciences journals. Some projects in the European Bioinformatics Institute also distributed how-to videos for tools such as Ensembl that is genome databases for vertebrates and other eukaryotic species, QuickGO that is a fast web-based browser for Gene Ontology (GO) terms and annotations, and GOA, Gene Ontology Annotation, that provides high-quality GO annotations to proteins in the UniProt Knowledgebase and International Protein Index.

Not only service providers in national institutes but also individual service providers including relatively small communities distributed tutorial videos. Galaxy, a collaboration system for genomic research, is a highly functional and complex system, but the procedure is easily understandable because the developers provide tutorial videos on their website. Taverna, which is an open source and domain-independent workflow management system (a suite of tools used to design and execute scientific workflows and aid *in silico* experimentation), is also described in the tutorials in a video format. ATTED-II, which provides co-regulated gene relationships to estimate gene function, has YouTube channel for tutorials. There are many video tutorials provided by the database and tool developers.

In addition, educators and users of web resources who do not develop any databases or tools also contribute to the scientific community by providing tutorial videos. BITS, Bioinformatics Tutorials Series, are a collaboration work of the MIT Engineering and Science Libraries and Harvard's Countway Library. BIREC, Bioinformatics Information Resource and eLearning Center, also provides tutorial videos. *OpenHelix* provides over 100 well-organized tutorial suites including videos on web-based bioinformatics and genomic resources. It also has many tutorial videos in 'Tip of this week' tagging articles in the blog section. In addition to videos provided by organizations, a YouTube search by database or tool name will provide many tutorial videos produced by volunteers.

Previous Section (http://bib.oxfordjournals.org/content/13/2/258.full#sec-3)

Next Section (http://bib.oxfordjournals.org/content/13/2/258.full#sec-13)

Togo TV: Online Tutorial Video Distribution Trial in Japan

To bridge the gap between service providers and users, we created and distributed tutorial videos of databases and web tools. We describe in this article, a methodology for making and distributing videos and elaborate on this methodology with examples. Togo TV ('Togo' means 'integration' in Japanese; pronunciation symbol is [toɯɡoɯ]) that is one of the services in the Integrated Database Project in Japan (Figure 1) is a portal site of tutorial and lecture videos about bioinformatics resources. Although the original Togo TV site is mostly written in Japanese, there is the English interface for international users. The site contains our original videos and third-party videos from publicly available website such as YouTube. All contents provided by us are distributed under the Creative Commons Attribution 2.1 Japan license and also provided as vodcasts that can be viewed using a portable device and on YouTube.

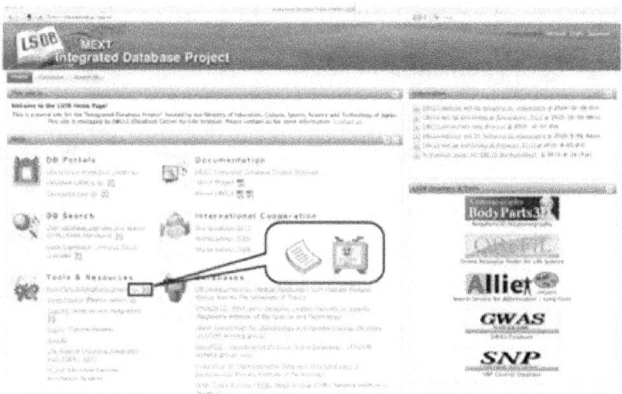

Figure 1: (http://bib.oxfordjournals.org/content/13/2/258.full#F1)

Although most of the contents are described in Japanese, there are 19 original programs in English, most of which explain a service developed in the Integrated Database Project such as TogoWS, which provides an integrated SOAP and REST APIs for interoperable bioinformatics Web services and OReFiL, which is an online resource finder for life science. We plan to expand our own English contents so as to enable our service to be used all over the world.

Screenshot of the MEXT Integrated Database Project portal (http://lifesciencedb.jp/en/). Paper icons and TV icons zoomed in the call-out following service names are linked to PDF documents and tutorial videos, respectively. MEXT, Ministry of Education, Culture, Sports, Science and Technology of Japan.

Currently, two types of video are provided: (i) tutorial videos of databases and tools (screencasts) and (ii) lecture videos of symposiums and workshops (live action). For screencast videos, a screen where the database or tools were operated was captured and edited using screencast software equipped with a caption-adding function, such as Camtasia Studio (TechSmith Corporation, Okemos, MI, USA) for Windows and DesktopToMovie (Pencil Software, Okinawa, Japan; only a Japanese-language version is available) for Mac. Recently, Camtasia: Mac (TechSmith Corporation) has been released, and we recommend its use rather than DesktopToMovie. For live-action videos, a lecture was recorded using a digital video camera or voice recorder, and then the source media was edited or embedded with presentation slides using tools such as Final Cut Pro (Apple Inc.) or iMovie (Apple Inc.). It is also possible to output presentations in Keynote (Apple Inc.) to videos. After capturing and editing, the source media was encoded in QuickTime format (.mov) and MPEG-4 format (.m4v) for distribution via websites and vodcast, respectively. The video compression type was set to H.264, and the sound format was specified to AAC if an audio track was included. For encoding in the QuickTime format, the 'Prepare for Internet Streaming' option was set to 'Fast Start' rather than 'Fast Start—Compressed Header' because the compressed header file format is impossible to play on Flash players. Other useful software packages for screencasting are listed in the article of Wikipedia entitled 'Comparison of screen casting software'.

To create user-friendly and high-quality tutorials, we suggest the following points: plan the tutorial; do a run-through before recording; edit adequately; pause at essential points; make the duration as short as possible and keep effects to a minimum. To capture a video smoothly, it is important to create a plan and run through it before recording. Editing costs may increase considerably if these preparatory steps are skipped. Here, editing involves deleting unnecessary frames and loading animation frames, thus ultimately reducing video downloading time, user viewing time and also file size. At key operating points, it is necessary to pause the animation; viewers need time to understand and absorb the information. In TogoTV videos, we insert a pause of about 5–10 s, depending on the situation. We also recommend that the video duration be made as short as possible and that animation effects be suppressed to a minimum. Most Togo TV contents fit in a 5-min video, except for lectures. Excessive production not only increases the production cost but also conceals the essence of the video. In general, since a dynamic video tends to increase file size, suppression of excessive animation will reduce the file size. Most video repositories have upload limitations based on video length and file size.

The most important thing when creating a video is to create a high-quality video that would be useful to viewers. When one creates video easily without any consideration of the quality of the product, it would be a waste of viewer's time and content creator's time and would add to the already overwhelming 'noise' of available training materials. Because both creating and viewing video are time consuming, one needs to create a video carefully. In a case of Togo TV, we have adopted an internal review in order to ensure quality. From planning to drafting, reviewing and publishing takes about a week in our case.

In May 2011, we have 310 tutorial videos in Togo TV (excluding lecture videos), and a total of 54 videos are updated ones.

Examples of tutorial videos in Togo TV

How to use BodyParts3D/anatomography

Anatomography is a 3D rendering tool for human anatomy and has been developed as part of the Integrated Database Project. A user can generate anatomical images by selecting body parts stored in the BodyParts3D database and setting their opacities, colors and viewpoint. The image is useful for communication between physicians and patients, and it can be generated as a heat map of the human body based on an organ name and a numeric value such as organ-specific gene expression data and cancer mortality. Figure 3A shows a screenshot of the BodyParts3D/anatomography tutorial video. This video describes how to build a 3D image, how to manipulate viewpoint and size, how to set opacities and colors and how to output to an image file. Videos of other services provided by the Integrated Database Project are also available at the project page. A TV icon after the service name (Figure 1) provides a link to a tutorial video.

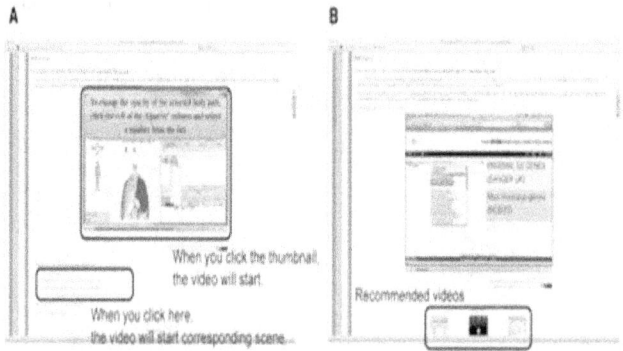

Figure 3: (http://bib.oxfordjournals.org/content/13/2/258.full#F3)

Screenshot of TogoTV's tutorial programs. Clicking the thumbnail in the center of the page will start the video. When the summary text of a video is clicked, the video will start the scene corresponding to the summary. There are links to recommended videos that are related playing video at the bottom of the page. (A) This video is entitled 'How to use BodyParts3D/Anatomography 2010'. (B) This video is entitled 'How to make probeID list for microarray using BioMart'.

How to use BioMart

We provide how-to videos of not only our own services but also useful tools all over the world. BioMart, a query-oriented data management system, is one of the most important tools in genome science. Users can submit various queries to retrieve lists of interest from BioMart. A screenshot of the tutorial video entitled 'How to make probeID list for microarray using BioMart' is shown in Figure 3B. In this video, the process for creating an ID conversion list for microarray analysis on the BioMart central portal website is introduced. From all genes in the mouse genome, genes that have corresponding entries in the Affymetrix mouse430 2 GeneChip are considered for further analysis. Genes with the Affymetrix GeneChip ID mentioned above are associated with the Agilent ProbeID and RefSeq ID via the Ensembl Gene ID. The results are downloadable in the tab separated value format with GNU-zip (.gzip) compression.

Lectures

Lectures are also distributed from Togo TV. Currently, we broadcast eight lectures in English. One is a video of a lecture about this service (Togo TV) held at the 2007 Annual

Conference of the Japanese Society for Bioinformatics (JSBi2007, Figure 4A). The second lecture is about Gendoo, a functional profiling tool for gene and disease features using the Mesh vocabulary, held at JSBi2008. The third is about copyright and data sharing in science entitled 'Copyright in the Digital Age and Its Impact on Scientific Data Sharing' by Professor Lawrence Lessig from Harvard Law School from the 'Balancing Intellectual Property Protection and Data Sharing in Science' symposium (Figure 4B). The others are about processing of large genomic data from 'Workshop on Parallel and Distributed Processing of Large Genome Data'.

A　　　　　　　　　　　**B**

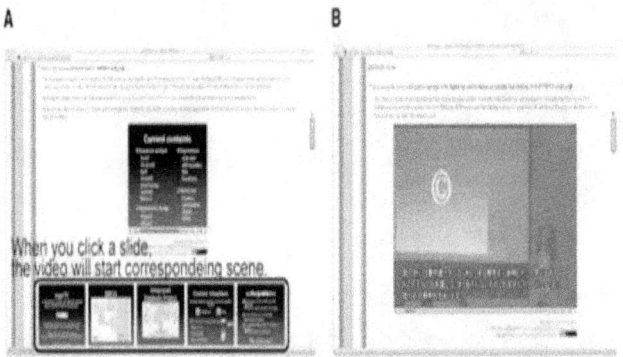

Figure 4: (http://bib.oxfordjournals.org/content/13/2/258.full#F4)

Screenshot of Togo TV's lecture programs. There are the slides appeared in the presentation at the bottom of the page. When you click a slide, the video will start corresponding scene. (A) Video of voice-over on slides. (B) Live-action video.

Statistics and user feedback

In May 2011, we provided over 450 videos, most of which are in Japanese. Togo TV is accessed 20 000 times per month from 5000 unique IP addresses and videos are played 4000 times per month. According to the analysis of IP addresses, accesses from '.jp' and '.com' domain accounted for about 33% and 31%, respectively. The rest included unknown domain (28%), '.net' (5%) and '.edu' (1%) domains. Although contents of Togo TV are mainly Japanese, there are accesses from outside of Japan. The analysis of access was carried out using AWStats, and we excluded the bot programs from the analysis. Videos accessed on YouTube measured through the YouTube API are played about 5000 times per month. Since Togo TV was started in July 2007, videos have been watched >250 000 times. The tutorial videos of basic tools and databases such as primer3, reactome, blast, clustalw, and Ensembl are the popular contents in TogoTV.

Reactions of most viewers are positive judging from the responses received during interviews at lectures and exhibitions. According to some instructors who used our videos for their bioinformatics lectures, their students' understanding increased considerably.

It is possible to provide tutorials in the video format because the continued development of computer hardware and software and the Internet. Various service developers have created and distributed tutorial videos via their own server or YouTube; our contribution was the launching of TogoTV, which provides over 450 videos and is one of the most active site collecting and maintaining tutorial videos. As pointed out by Williams *et al.*, tutorial videos are not always in depth enough to provide a full understanding of the resource to users. But it is effective for them to touch on use of web resources. Further development of computer and web infrastructure will accelerate this movement in the future.

It would be helpful if database and tool developers publish how-to videos as well as documents to encourage greater use. Even if one is just a user of web resources and not a service developer or provider, the creation and distribution of a tutorial video based on experience is useful for numerous researchers. The most important thing is to create a high-quality video that would be useful to viewers. To show summary text, captions and dialogues of a video as well as description is also useful in determining whether or not to watch the video. The creation of tutorial videos in a community is particularly useful for sharing and standardizing the annotation and curation process.

We believe that providing tutorial videos created by database and tool providers as well as users will promote research activities and help to distribute the knowledge of database and tool handling in research communities. Thus, we propose that everyone who produces and uses web resources create tutorial videos and share them.

Key Points

1) Improvements of computer technology and the Internet enable creation and distribution of a tutorial video easily.

2) Some major database and tool developers provided tutorial videos via their website and/or YouTube.

3) We developed TogoTV, a website where tutorial videos of bioinformatics databases, tools and lectures are distributed, and this attempt acquired a good reputation.

4) Let us create and share tutorial videos all together.

Source: (http://www.oxfordjournals.org/our_journals/bib/terms.html).

IMP-BIOINFO-SOLUTIONS

(http://www.thebioinformatica.com/onlinetutorial.htm)

DUMMIES

(http://spdbv.vital-it.ch/TheMolecularLevel/Matics/)

Chapter 5: BIOINFORMATICS BLOGS

The following blog sites offer a wide range of news and views on a diversity of biosciences-related topics from individuals ranging from graduate students to established principal investigators and science writers.

The rankings provided reflect a composite of the quality and quantity of content on the blog site as well as how directly related they are to the focus of Kinetica Online. If you are aware of any other blog sites that should be included here, please contact kinetica@kinexus.ca.

List of Bioinformatics Blogs

Site	Rating	Description
123 bioinformatics (http://forum.123bioinformatics.com/)	*	A blog site with over 1167 biotechnology help topics but these often relate to non-scientific issues.
All-wow videos- Mass Spectrometry (http://www.wowtube.ru/index.php?key=Spectrometry)	**	Over 50 short videos related to mass spectrometry. The Wow sites also provide instructional videos on a wide range of other topics.
American Biotechnologist (http://www.americanbiotechnologist.com/blog/)	**	This blog from Bio-Rad (Hercules, CA) has been created as a place where PIs, Graduate Students, Technicians and Science Educators can network, post and view articles, videos, seminars, techniques etc of interest and generally find subject matter relevant to them.

Site	Rating	Description
Aetiology (http://scienceblogs.com/aeti	**	A personal blog site from Dr. Tara Smith, who is an assistant professor of

ology/)		Epidemiology in Iowa, which focuses on the causes, origins, evolution and implication of disease and other phenomena.
Bad Science (http://www.badscience.net/)	**	A personal blog site from Dr. Ben Goldacre, who is a medical doctor, writer and broadcaster. Bad Science covers a wide range of health and science topics.
Becker (http://beaker.sanfordburnham.org/)	**	A blog site produced by Sanford-Burnham Medical Research Institute (La Jolla, CA) that covers recent medical research with commentaries from diverse individuals.
Bench Marks (http://www.chhblogs.org/cshprotocols/category/proteins-and-proteomics/)	***	The focus of this blog is the discussion of methods used in biology laboratories. This blog is kept by David Crotty, the Executive Editor of Cold Spring Harbor Protocols (Woodbury, NY).
Beyond The Human Eye (http://beyondthehumaneye.blogspot.in/)	***	A personal blog site from Phil Gates, a botanist at Durham University, on botanist at Durham University, with commentaries and outstanding microphoto images on microbiology topics.

Site	Rating	Description
BioBOOM -The Biotech Blog (http://bioboom.blogspot.in/)	***	A blog site produced by Yali Friedman and focuses on the business of biotechnology with news of medical breakthroughs and the biopharma industry.

Biochemistry and Bioinformatics (http://biosiva.blogspot.in/ 2010_01_01_archive.html)	**	This website features diverse articles on biochemistry and bioinformatics and is produced by the Sri Sankara Arts and Science College (Enathur, Kanchipuram).
Biocrowd (http://www.biocrowd.com/)	**	BioCrowd is an on-line social network started by Drs. Clifford S. Mintz and Vincent Racaniello and designed for interactions between individuals involved and interested in the biosciences. Professionals. It features only very recent blogs.
Biohacker (https://biohacker.wordpress .com/)	**	This website is produced by a physicist identified as Dimitri that is learning biochemistry.
Biohealth Investor (http://biohealthinvestor.com /)	*	A commercial blog site from Biohealth Investor (New Rochelle, NY) that provides daily updates on companies and trends in the biotech industry.
BioImplement (http://bioimplement.blogspo t.in/)	*	A personal blog site from Christopher Hogue (Singapore) that has not been updated since Feb. 2009.

Site	Rating	Description
Bioinfoblog (http://bioinfoblog.it/)	*	Not too many blogs on this website from Italy with infrequent updates.
Bioinformatics Organization (http://www.bioinformatics.or g/)	*	The website for the Bioinformatics Organization with news and commentaries.
Bioinformatics SnowDeal	*	A personal blog site from Eric C.

Site	Rating	Description
(http://bioinformatics.snowdeal.org/)		Snowdeal III devoted to bioinformatics. However, it has not been updated since June 2006.
Bioinformatics: biology by other means (http://blogs.scientifik.info/bioinformatics/?cat=3)	*	A personal blog site from Alberto Labarga (Granada, Spain) that has not been since Oct. 2009.
Bioinformatics@Becker (http://beckerinfo.net/bioinformatics/)	**	A blog site with updates and Musings from the Bioinformatics team at Becker Medical Library.
Biology in Science Fiction (http://blog.sciencefictionbiology.com/)	**	A personal blog site produced by Peggy discusses cloning, genetic engineering, mutant monsters, longevity treatments and all the other biology behind science fiction.
BioMed Central Blog (http://blogs.biomedcentral.com/bmcblog/)	***	This website produced by BioMEd Central features articles on diverse topics in biology.

Site	Rating	Description
Biopharmconsortium Blog (http://www.biopharmconsortium.com/blog/)	**	A commercial blog site from Allan B. Haberman (Wayland, MA) on various biotechnology advances.
Bioscience Technology (http://www.biosciencetechnology.com/blogs)	*	A blog site from Bioscience Technology with commentaries related to biological sciences and biotechnology.

Biosearch Tech Blog (http://blog.biosearchtech.com/)	**	This website from the company Biosearch Technologies and covers diagnostics methodologies.
Bio-Synthesis (http://bio-synthesis.blogspot.in/)	*	A commercial blog site from Bio-Synthesis, Inc. that appears to mainly profile their products.
Biotech Blog (http://www.biotechblog.com/)	**	A blog site produced by Yali Friedman (Washington, DC) has commentaries on commercial, legal, political and scientific trends in biotechnology.
BIOtechNOW (http://www.biotech-now.org/)	**	BIOtechNOW (Mississauga, Ontario) seeks to contribute to public conversation about the impact of biotechnology on our lives and our world. It explores how biotechnology helps heal, fuel, and feed our global community through sound, video, and the printed word. It is produced by the Biotechnology Industry Organization (BIO).

Site	Rating	Description
BioTuesdays (http://biotuesday.ca/)	**	A blog site produced by Leonard Zehr and Stephen Kilmer tracks developments in healthcare companies, particularly in Canada.
Biowizard (http://biotuesday.ca/)	**	This website features a wide range of articles and is sponsored by Chemblog and Sigma (Wayne, PA).
BioWorld	***	BioWorld Today is a daily source of news

(http://www.bioworld.com/)		about developments in companies in the biotechnology industry. Subscription required.
Bitesize bio (http://bitesizebio.com/303/kinase-structures-and-autoinhibition/)	**	Bitesize Bio is an online magazine and community for molecular and cell biology researchers.
Blind.Scientist (http://blindscientist.genedrift.org/)	*	A personal blog site from a bioinformaticist with very brief musings on bioinformatics and other science topics.
Blog.Bioethics.Net (http://www.bioethics.net/)	***	This website from the editors of the American Journal of Bioethics is dedicated to the study and teaching of ethical dimensions of health care and health policy.
Blogged (http://blogged.com/)	**	An expansive website that covers diverse topics. The website's search engine provides for the retrieval of news and blogs on more specific subjects including cell biology and biochemistry.

Site	Rating	Description
Blogging the Business of Biotech (http://insidebioia.com/)	***	This website produced by the Biotechnology Industry Organization features updates on biotech companies and the biotechnology industry.
Blogtoplist (http://www.blogtoplist.com/rss/)	**	An expansive website that covers diverse topics. The website's directory provides for the retrieval of blogs based on categories that are located

		in alphabetical order.
Boston Blog (http://blogs.nature.com/bosto n/ 2007/07/26/combining-cell-biology-with-cinema)	**	This website features news and commentary on the Boston science scene.
Business, bytes, genes, molecules (http://blog.deepaksingh.net/)	***	A personal blog site from Deepak Singh with commentaries on science, data and computing.
Canadian BioTechnologist2.0 (https://cbt20.wordpress.com/)	***	A commercial website from Bio-Rad that features contributions from undergraduate and post-graduate students, bench scientists, and technologists that includes posters, tools, research, presentations, articles, white papers, multimedia, music downloads and entertainment, conference announcements, and videos.

Site	Rating	Description
Cell Biology (http://cellbiology.newshee t. com/category/Cell_Biology _Blogs)	**	Cell Biology Newsbeet is social news, blog and bookmarking site where people can discuss all about blogs, news and information of Cell Biology.
Chemblogs (http://www.chemblogs.co m/?f)	**	A commercial blog site from Sigma-Aldrich as a feedback panel for the global chemical community, with posts written by Sigma-Aldrich personnel and invited posts from leaders in academia and industry.

ChEMBL-og (http://chembl.blogspot.in/)	**	A blog site from the Computational Chemical Biology Group (ChEMBL) based at the EMBL-EBI Outstation at Hinxton, U.K. It covers news and progress related to drug discovery and provides access to databases.
Chemical blog space (http://cb.openmolecules.net/ blogs.php?category=Biochemistry)	*	A blog site with relatively few comments actually linked to chemistry.
Clinical Cases and Images: Caseblog (http://casesblog.blogspot.in/)	**	A website with health news updated by an assistant professor at the University of Chicago.
Comprendia (http://comprendia.com/ category/blog/)	*	A commercial blog site produced by Mary Canady with suggestions for marketing to life science companies.

Site	Rating	Description
Comprendia Blog (http://comprendia.com/ category/blog/)	**	This website produced by the Compendia Biosciences Consulting Group and contains commentary on effective marketing.
Confessions of a (former) Lab Rat (http://occamstypewriter.org/rpg/)	**	A personal blog site from Richard P. Grant of the Nature Publishing Group, which focuses on diverse science
Corante - In the Pipeline (http://pipeline.corante.com/archive	**	A personal blog site from Dr. Derek Lowe, who is an organic

s/ 2006/02/12/kinase_inhibitors_doomed_from_the_start.php)		chemist that has worked a several major pharmaceutical companies. Corante presents through the eyes of leading observers, analysts, thinkers, and doers, critical themes and memes in technology, business, law, science, and culture.
Culture Dish (http://scienceblogs.com/culturedish/)	**	A personal blog site from science writer Rebecca Skloot about diverse topics in science and medicine.
Daily Tech (http://www.dailytech.com/New+DNA+Microarray+Technique+Based+on+Electrostatics/article12233.htm)	*	A website with daily broad technology news and commentary. Biomedical related topics appear every two to three weeks.

Site	Rating	Description
Developing Intelligence (http://scienceblogs.com/developingintelligence/)	**	A personal blog site from Chris Chatham, a graduate student at the University of Colorado (Boulder, CO) with a focus on developmental and computational cognitive neuroscience, comparative psychology, psychometrics and artificial intelligence.
DNA bloggers (https://twitter.com/DNAbloggers)	*	A blog site with commentaries on genomics-related topics, but not very recent (San Francisco, CA).
DNA exchange (http://thednaexchange.com/	**	A blog site with commentaries from a group of genetic counselors with an

)		interest in public discussion of genetics-related issues.
Ensembl Weblog (http://ensembl.blogspot.in/)	*	The Ensemble Weblog contains information on updates to databases in Ensembl (UK).
Experimental Man Project (http://www.technologyrevie w.com/ contributor/david-ewing-duncan/)	**	A blog site with genomics and disease commentaries from David Ewing Duncan, who is a journalist and author, and the Director of the Center for Life Science Policy at UC Berkeley.
Eye on DNA (http://www.eyeondna.com/)	**	A blog site with commentary from Dr. Hsien-Hsien Lei and videos related to DNA.

Site	Rating	Description
FuturePundit (http://www.futurepundit.com/)	**	A blog site with commentary from Randall Parker and news about future technological trends and their likely effects on human society, politics and evolution.
GEN (http://www.genengnews.com/ 500.aspx?aspxerrorpath=/pub lic/ blog/default.aspx)	***	The blog site for Genetic Engineering and Biotech News.
Gene Dog Blog (http://genedog.com/blog/ 2009/06/jmcb/)	**	A personal blog site from Gerry Gao (a biological science student of Shanghai Jiao Tong University, China) with a focus on Developmental Biology.
Gene Expression	***	A personal blog site from Razib Khan

(http://scienceblogs.com/gnxp/)		that features a wide variety of comments related to the biological sciences including book reviews.
Gene Forum (http://www.geneforum.org/blog)	***	Geneforum is a nonprofit affiliate of the Portland State University Foundation created in 1998 to "promote dialogue at the intersection of genetics, ethics, and public values."
Gene Sherpas (http://www.thegenesherpa.blogspot.in/)	***	A blog site produced by Dr. Steve Murphy (New York, NY) with commentary on medical genetics and personalized medicine.

Site	Rating	Description
Genetic Future (http://scienceblogs.com/geneticfuture/)	***	A blog site with commentary from Dr. Daniel MacArthur (New York, NY) on human genetics and personal genomics.
Genetic Interference (http://www.genetic-inference.co.uk/)	**	A blog site with commentary on disease genetics, genomics, statistics and public health, as well as communication of science by Luke Jostins, a Graduate Student at King�s College, Cambridge and the Sanger Institute.
Genetic Engineering & Biotechnology News (http://www.genengnews.com/)	**	A website that includes web-exclusive news and features, Webinars, videos, podcasts, and newsletters related to the biomedical advances and the biotechnology industry.
GeneticsBlogs	**	This blog is dedicated to the subject of

(http://geneticsblogs.com/)		Genetics and DNA Testing and includes commentaries and videos.
Genome Alberta Blogs (http://genomealberta.ca/blogs /)	***	This website is a source of information related to genomics, proteomics, bioinformatics and bioethics research in Alberta. It is based on the main website of Genome Alberta (Calgary, Alberta).
Genomes Unzipped (http://genomesunzipped.org/)	**	Genomes Unzipped is a group blog providing expert, independent commentary on the personal genomics industry.

Site	Rating	Description
Genomeweb (https://www.genomeweb.co m/)	****	This website provides a daily listing of news from the biotechnology industry and advances in biomedical research (New York, USA).
Genomeweb - The Daily Scan (https://www.genomeweb.co m/scan)	****	This website provides a daily listing of interesting blogs from a wide range of other blog sites (New York, USA).
Genomicron (http://www.genomicron. evolverzone.com/)	**	A personal blog site with commentary from T. Ryan Gregory, an evolutionary biologist specializing in genome size evolution at the University of Guelph in Canada.
Genomics Law Report (http://www.genomicslawrep ort. com/)	**	Genomics Law Report is a publication of the law firm Robinson, Bradshaw & Hinson focusing on the legal implications of important developments

		in the fields of genomics and personalized medicine.
Health Blog (http://blogs.wsj.com/health/ 2008/ 06/17/mixed-results- for-experimental-alzheimers- antibody/)	***	Health Blog offers news and analysis on health and the business of health. The blog is written by Katherine Hobson and includes contributions from staffers at The Wall Street Journal, WSJ.com and Dow Jones Newswire.
Here Be Answers (http://www.herebeanswers. com/ p/links-to-all-posts-on- here-be-answers.html)	**	A website that contains answers to a wide range of interesting questions in science, technology and business.

Site	Rating	Description
HPC info (http://hpcinfo.com/)	**	A website produced by Gary Stiehr with information and discussion about High Performance Computing as largely applied to genomics.
IamBiotech (http://www.biotech- now.org/)	***	A blog site produced by produced by the Biotechnology Industry Organization (BIO) that is dedicated to helping the biotech community address those challenges and support the industry's work to Heal, Fuel and Feed the world.
iBiome (http://ibiome.typepad.com/)	*	A personal blog site from Brain Yates with commentary on general biology topics.
IguanaBio (http://www.iguanabio.com/)	**	This website is a daily pharma and biotech tabloid that takes a colorful and unique perspective on the industry's breaking news, developments, events

		and personalities.
IVDTinsight (http://www.ivdtechnology.com/blog)	**	IVD Technology is a trade journal designed for manufacturers of in vitro diagnostic products with peer-reviewed articles covering a wide range of technical and regulatory topics. The publications primary focus is on diagnostics technologies--including research, development, and manufacturing.

Site	Rating	Description
JCVI Weblog (http://blogs.jcvi.org/)	***	A blog site produced by the J. Craig Venter Institute (Rockville, MD) that has news and articles related to genomics studies.
Jim's Corner (http://www.biotech-now.org/jims-corner)	**	A personal blog site that features the thoughts and perspectives from the Biotechnology Industry Organization's president and CEO Jim Greenwood.
Kosmix (http://health.kosmix.com/)	**	An expansive website with news and views on diverse subjects, including health care and science.
Lab Manager Editor's Buzz (http://www.labmanager.com/blogs/Editor)	**	A blog site edited by Pam Ahlberg (Midland, ON) with commentary about laboratory technology, research news and trends, and events.
LC Sciences Blog (http://www.lcsciences.com/bl	**	A commercial blog site from LC Sciences website (Houston, TX).

og/)		
Lymphoma Info (http://www.lymphomainfo.net/ blog)	**	A blog site that covers lymphoma-related issues by providing concise, up-to-date information and a meeting place for lymphoma patients and those who care about them.

Site	Rating	Description
Mass Genomics (http://massgenomics.org/)	**	A personal blog site that features comments about genomics from Dan Koboldt, who works in the Medical Genomics group of the Genome Sequencing Center at Washington University in St. Louis.
Mass Spectrometry Blog (http://mass-spec.lsu.edu/blog/)	**	A Web log of mass spectrometry websites, discussion groups, mailing lists and other links and items of interest to the mass spectrometry community. This blog is run by Kermit Murray, professor of chemistry at Louisiana State University.
Mayo Clinic (http://www.mayoclinic.org/ diseases-conditions)	***	This website contains a wealth of information, including questions and answers about many different diseases (Rochester, MN).
Medchem Blog (http://medchemblog.blogspot.in /)	**	This blog site provides information on drug discovery related topics such as medicinal chemistry and pharmacological aspects of drugs as

		well as simple lab techniques.
Medical Blogs (http://blogs.jwatch.org/)	**	This website includes medical-related blogs that are tracked by Journal Watch.

Site	Rating	Description
Medical News, Articles and Blogs (http://www.medinews.co.uk/ forum)	**	This website features medical news, articles and blogs with several medical-focused forums.
MedWorm-Bioinformatics Blog (http://www.medworm.com/ rss/blogs.php)	**	This blog site features a wide range of medical focused forums with blogs from other blog sites.
Microarray BiochipTechnology (http://arrayit.blogspot.in/)	*	A commercial blog site from Arrayit Corporation and Todd Martinsky covering microarray technology advancements.
Microarray Blog (https://microarray.wordpres s.com/ feed/)	**	A blog site with commentary and news from Albin Paul on microaray technology and other biotechnology.
Microbial Art (http://www.microbialart.com /)	***	A website that features a collection of unique artworks created using living bacteria, fungi, and protists.
Microbiology Blog (http://www.horizonpress.co m/ blogger/)	**	A blog site with microbiology news and views that focuses on journal articles and book reviews (UK).
MicrobiologyBytes	**	A blog site produced by Dr. Alan Cann

(https://microbiologybytes. wordpress.com/)		with news and comments related to microbiology topics.

Site	Rating	Description
miRNA blog (http://mirnablog.com/)	**	A blog site dedicated to tracking advances in the microRNA field with news, commentaries and blogs.
Molecular Biology Blog (http://www.horizonpress.com/ blogger/)	**	A blog site with commentary on current research, forthcoming conferences, hot research topics, high impact publications (UK).
My Biotech Life (http://my.biotechlife.net/)	**	A blog site with commentary by Ricardo Vidal about life sciences and biotechnology topics.
Nascent (http://blogs.nature.com/nasce nt/)	**	A commercial blog site from the Nature Publishing Grioup on web technology and science.
Nature.com ZBlogs (http://blogs.nature.com/)	***	A websire with blogs written by the editors and journalists and members of Nature Network and also includes posts from hundreds of third party science blogs.
Neurologica Blog (http://theness.com/ neurologicablog/)	***	A personal blog site from Dr.Steven Novella, who is an academic clinical neurologist at Yale University School of Medicine. His blog covers news and issues in neuroscience, but also general science, scientific skepticism, philosophy of science, critical thinking,

		and the intersection of science with the media and society.

Site	Rating	Description
Neurophilosophy (http://scienceblogs.com/ neurophilosophy/)	***	A personal blog site produced by a molecular and developmental neurobiologist turned science writer.
Nex-Gen Sequencing (http://nextgenseq.blogspot.in/)	***	A blog site from Stuart Brown, an associate professor in the Dept. of Cell Biology at NYU School of Medicine, which focuses on the rapidly developing world of Next-Generation DNA sequencing, with an emphasis on bioinformatics.
NSGC President's Blog (http://nsgcpresident.blogspot.in /)	**	A personal blog site from Liz Kearney, who is the President of National Society of Genetic Counsellors (NSGC). The blog covers topics related to the interests of NSGC.
Omics! Omics! (http://omicsomics.blogspot.in/)	**	A personal blog site from Dr. Keith Robinson, a computational biologist, on new technologies, genomics and proteomics.
PCR blog (http://www.highveld.com/pcr/)	*	A blog site with information on PCR reviews, PCR technology, tips and advice, and troubleshooting (UK).

Site	Rating	Description
PepCyber (http://www.pepcyber.org/PPEP/)	****	PepCyber: P~Pep is the largest public database of human protein-protein interactions mediated by phosphoprotein binding domains (PPBDs). The database is hand curated from peer-reviewed literature and is a rich information source emphasizing the reported, experimentally validated data for specific PPBD-PPEP interactions. The current release of the PepCyber: P~Pep database V1.2 (May 2010) includes 11,269 records of interactions between 387 PPBD proteins and 1,471 substrate proteins, curated from 4,852 publi
Pharma Strategy Blog (http://www.pharmastrategyblog.com/)	**	A commercial blog site from Dr. Sally Church of Icarus Consultants, Inc., with a focus on developments in oncology, haematology, immunology, respiratory and HIV.
PIMM - Partial Immortalization (https://pimm.wordpress.com/2008/04/23/human-proteome-project-21000-genes1-protein-10-years-1-billion/)	*	A personal blog site from Attila Chordash, who is a molecular biologist and biotechnologist. His blog site covers personal genetics, stem cells and mitochondria, regenerative medicine, biotechnology, indefinite life extension, science hacks and bioDIY amongst others.

Site	Rating	Description

Plant Biotech Blog (http://www.plantbiotechblog.com/)	**	A personal blog site from Dr. Chavali Kameswara Rao, who is a professor in the Department of Sericulture at the Bangalore University in Bangalore, India. Plant Biotech Blog features analyses and views on various issues of modern agricultural biotechnology.
PMC Blog (https://ageofpersonalizedmedicine.wordpress.com/)	***	A blog site with commentaries from the Personalized Medicine Coalition.
PollTiGenomics (http://www.politigenomics.com/)	**	PollTiGenomics is a blog by David Dooling about the confluence (and sometimes incongruence) of several of the most important topics surrounding the future of human health: genomics, information technology, and politics.
PolitiGenomics (http://www.politigenomics.com/)	**	A personal blog site from David Dooling, who runs the Analysis Developers, Laboratory Information Management Systems (LIMS), and the Information Systems groups at The Genome Center at Washington University in St. Louis School of Medicine. PolitiGenomics is devoted to commentary about the confluence (and sometimes incongruence) of several of the most important topics surrounding the future of human health: genomics, information technology, and politics.

Site	Rating	Description
Proteomics 2.0	**	A blog and discussion forum from the

Site	Rating	Description
(http://www.proteomics2.com/)		compant SageN Research, Inc. for tools, insights and approaches for the next generation of proteomics analysis.
Public Rambling (http://www.evocellnet.com/p/ research.html)	**	A personal blog site from Dr. Pedro Beltrao with comments on bioinformatics science and technology.
Red Orbit (http://www.redorbit.com/ news/health/)	**	A website with news on a wide diversity of science and technology-related subjects as well as education, entertainment, business, politics and sports (Texas).
Regina's Biology Blog (http://biology.about.com/)	**	A personal blog site from Regina Lynn Bailey, who is a science educator, with news and comments related to scientific insights in biology and health.
Research Blog (http://researchblogging.org/)	**	A website that links to blog sites on diverse subjects in science and the humanities.
RNA bioinformatics (http://www.rnabioinformatics.org/)	**	A personal blog site from Yi Xing, an Assistant Professor in the Department of Internal Medicine and Department of Biomedical Engineering, University of Iowa. It focuses on genomics and bioinformatics but has not been updated since 2007.

Site	Rating	Description
Sandwalk (http://sandwalk.blogspot.in/)	**	A personal blog site from Dr. Laurence Moran, who is a biochemistry professor at the University of Toronto.

Sci Blogs (http://sciblogs.co.nz/code-for-life/2010/03/21/bioinformatics-blog-carnival/)	**	A personal blog site from a computational biologist that covers a wide range of science-related topics (New Zealand).
Science 2.0 (http://www.science20.com/all_blogs)	**	This website features news and commentaries on a wide range of life and physical science-, medicine- and social sciences-related topics.
Science Base Blog (http://www.sciencebase.com/ science-blog/)	***	This general science website produced by David Bradley features science news, interviews and commentaries.
Science Blog (http://scienceblog.com/)	***	A large blogsite with news and commentaries on general science.
Science Blogs (http://scienceblogs.com/channel/life-science/?utm_source=globalChannel&utm_medium=link)	***	A website with news and commentary on a wide range of topics in the life sciences.

Site	Rating	Description
Science Careers Blog (http://sciencecareers.sciencemag.org/career_magazine)	**	This blog site from Science Magazine provides updates from the science-career trenches including advice, opinion, news, funding opportunities, and links to other career-related resources.

Science Life (http://sciencelife.uch ospitals.edu/ tag/cell/)	**	This blog site is produced by Jeremy Manier and Rob Mitchum at the University of Chicago Medical Center and provides news and commentary about clinical and theoretical advances ◆ from new kinds of cancer treatments to new ideas about how life evolved. Contributors to the blog include some of the world◆s leading authorities on complex surgery, cancer, evolution, genetics, heart disease, organ transplants, and many other fields.
Science Roll (http://scienceroll.com /)	**	A website produced by Dr. Bertalan Mesko (Hungary) with commentaries and other features related to genomics and medicine.
Science-based Medicine (http://www.scienceba sedmedicine. org/)	**	This blog site explores issues and controversies in the relationship between science and medicine. The editorial staffs of Science-Based Medicine is composed of physicians who, alarmed at the manner in which unscientific and pseudoscientific health care ideas have increasingly infiltrated academic medicine and medicine at large, have decided to do their part to examine these claims in the light of science and scepticism.

Site	Rating	Description
Scienceforums (http://www.scienceforums.n et/)	**	This website features a large variety of forms with thousands of blogs on different subjects including science and medicine.
Scientist Solutions (http://www.scientistsolution	***	This website features a large variety of forms with news and commentaries on

s.com/ science-forum.aspx)		different techniques and equipment used in biomedical research.
Sigma Bioblogs (http://www.sigmabioblogs.com/)	*	This commercial blog site from Sigma Life Science with comments primarily about products and services for biomedical research.
Spoonful of Medicine (http://blogs.nature.com/spoonful/)	**	This blog site produced by the Nature Group contains commentaries on science, medicine and politics.
Stem Cell Daily (http://stemcelldaily.com/)	**	This website is collection of news articles about stem cells and research.
Steve's Systems Biology Blog (http://www.stevecheckley.co.uk/ blog/)	*	A personal blog site from Steve Checkley, who is a Ph.D. graduate student in systems biology at the University of Manchester (UK).
Target Health Global (http://blog.targethealth.com/?p=11815)	**	A commercial website produced by Target Health Inc. with news and videos about biomedical advances (New York, NY).

Site	Rating	Description
The Bioinformatics Blog (http://bioinformatics.whatheblog. com/)	**	A blog site with commentaries from volunteer writers and Bioinformaticists from around the world.
The Biotech Ethics Blog (http://biotechethicsblog.com/)	**	This blog site produced by Dr. Chris MacDonald is focused on ethical issues in the biotechnology industry, including health biotech, food biotech, and

Site	Rating	Description
		industrial biotech.
The Cross-border Biotech Blog (http://crossborderbiotech.ca /)	*	This blog site edited by Dr. Jeremy Grushcow covers developments in the biotech industry in Canada, the U.S. and abroad.
The Evilutionary Biologist (http://evilutionarybiologist. blogspot.in/)	**	A personal blog site from John Dennehy, an evolutionary biologist affiliated with Queens College and the CUNY Graduate Center.
The Genetic Genealogist (http://www.thegeneticgenea logist. com/)	**	A blog site produced by Blaine Bettinger that seeks to examine the intersection of traditional genealogical techniques and modern genetic research. The blog also explores the latest news and developments in the related field of personal genomics.
The Genetic Link (http://blog.dnagenotek.com/ blogdnagenotekcom)	*	This is commercial blog site from DNA Genotek that is focused on providing new insights about DNA and RNA sample collection.

Site	Rating	Description
The Great Beyond (http://blogs.nature.com/new s/ category/biology-biotechnology)	**	A Nature Group blog site that focuses on biology and biotechnology.
The Haystack (http://cenblog.org/the-haystack)	**	A blog site from Central Science that features news and commentary on chemistry and life sciences advances.
The Health Care Blog	***	This website features news about health

(http://thehealthcareblog.com/)		care advances and includes interviews and videos. It prints original material from many contributors and syndicates posts from other bloggers.
The In Vivo Blog (http://invivoblog.blogspot.in/)	***	This website, produced by Elsevier Business Intelligence. features daily news about medical advances and is
The Loom (http://blogs.discovermagazine.com/ loom/)	**	A blog site from science writer Carl Zimmer provides news and commentary on diverse science-related subjects.
The Microarray Blog (http://microarray.scienceboard.net/)	*	A blog site produced in collaboration between the Science Advisory Board and Albin Paul, who is a pharmacologist, is a focus on who enjoys the fields of drug discovery & development and bioinformatics; and in particular, microarray technology. The site does not seem to be recently updated.

Site	Rating	Description
The Open Helix Blog (http://blog.openhelix.com/)	**	A blog site with commentary and news from Jennifer and other staff at Open Helix.
The Personal Genome (http://thepersonalgenome.com/)	**	This website features commentaries and short video interviews on genomics and personalized medicine. It is produced by Jason Bobe, who is the Director of Community for the Personal Genome Project based out of George Church◆s lab at Harvard

		Medical School.
The Science Advisory Board (http://www.scienceboard.org/ community/blogs.asp)	*	A website that links to a series of blog sites produced in collaboration with The Science Advisory Board. It aims to improve communications between medical and life science professionals and the companies who provide this community with products and services.
The Weblog Biotech (http://www.biotech-weblog.com/)	***	A blog site produced by Creative Weblogging that covers advances in medicine and biotechnology.
Think Gene (http://www.thinkgene.com/)	**	A bio blog produced by Josh Hill and Kevin Fischer about genetics, genomics, and biotechnology.

Site	Rating	Description
Thoughtomics (http://www.lucasbrouwers.nl/blog / 2010/04/phosphorylation-without-a-cause/)	**	A personal blog site from Lucas Brouwers, who is a M.Sc. student in Molecular Mechanisms of Disease in Nijmegen (Netherlands). The blog provides commentary on evolution, bioinformatics, music and assorted random thoughts.
Transcription and Translation (http://scienceblogs.com/transcript/)	**	A personal blog site from Dr. Alex Palazzo, an assistant professor in Biochemistry at the University of Toronto, which focuses on mRNA,

		cell biology and related topics.
Tree of Life (http://feeds.feedburner.com/ phylogenomics)	**	A personal blog site produced by Jonathan Eisen, an evolutionary biologist at the University of California, Davis.
UTNE Blogs (http://www.utne.com/blogs/blog-landing.aspx)	**	A broad website that covers everything from the science and technology to the environment to the economy, politics to pop culture.
Virology Blog (http://www.virology.ws/)	**	A personal blog site from Dr. Vincent Racaniello, a Professor of Microbiology at Columbia University Medical Center, that provides educational insights into viruses and viral diseases.

Site	Rating	Description
What You're Doing Is Rather Desperate (https://nsaunders.wordpres s.com/)	**	A personal blog site from Neil Saunders, a statistical bioinformatician with CSIRO Mathematics, Information and Statistics, with a focus on genome-scale analysis and the computational tools.
Wikio-Biochemistry (http://www.wikio.co.uk/)	*	Wikio is a personalisable news page featuring a news search engine that searches media sites, blogs and the contributions of Wikio members.
Wired Science (http://www.wired.com/categ ory/ wiredscience)	***	This website produced by Wired Magazine contains general science articles.

Yokofakun (http://plindenbaum.blogspot.in/)	**	A personal blog site from bioinformaticist Dr. Pierre Lindenbaum (Paris, France) about bioinformatics, semantic web, comics and social networks.

Wiki Pathways

The PCBC Bioinformatics Core is posting a series of tutorials that will walk researchers through the process of creating reference digital pathways for analysis with their own omics data and those produced by the Cincinnati Cell Characterization Core (C4). It is recommended that people view these tutorials and follow along prior to group pathway creation or editing sessions. All videos are open-access.

A basic introduction for creating a WikiPathway from an existing progenitor differentiation pathway figure is shown in the below video. This video walks the user through downloading PathVisio, finding the pathway, entering the gene IDs into PathVisio, making a nicely curated pathway and uploading it to WikiPathway, Creating a Lineage Specification Pathway in Pathvisio (TBA) (http://youtu.be/ GRtaLihkTGM).

Translational Medicine & Human Health

(http://beckerinfo.net/bioinformatics/translational-medicine-human-health/): The AAAS Center for Public Engagement with Science and Technology just released a great set of lectures on translational medicine. The lectures are part of the Abelson Advancing Science Seminar Series.

NIH Video casts

(http://beckerinfo.net/bioinformatics/nih-videocasts/): Have you had an opportunity to check out the videocasts from NIH? The Center for Information Technology (CIT) makes special NIH events, seminars, and lectures available to viewers on the NIH network and the Internet from the VideoCast web site. There are a wide variety of topics offered and this is a great opportunity to [...] (http://beckerinfo.net/bioinformatics/nih-videocasts/).

National Library of Medicine update

(http://beckerinfo.net/bioinformatics/nlmnews/): Some interesting news was given by Medical Library Association (MLA) during the National Library of Medicine (NLM) update. Dr. Lindberg discussed the increasing need for libraries to play a role in supporting clinical trials and he also discussed disaster preparedness efforts at NLM. Coverage given on bioinformatics (http://beckerinfo.net/bioinformatics/category/ bioinformatics/) database (http://beckerinfo.net/bioinformatics/category/ database/), event

(http://beckerinfo.net/bioinformatics/category/event/),   Information
(http://beckerinfo.net/bioinformatics/category/information/),   NCBI
(http://beckerinfo.net/bioinformatics/category/ncbi/),   NLM
(http://beckerinfo.net/bioinformatics/category/nlm/),   resources
(http://beckerinfo.net/bioinformatics/category/resources/),   science
(http://beckerinfo.net/bioinformatics/category/science/),   tutorial
(http://beckerinfo.net/bioinformatics/category/tutorial/),   webinar
(http://beckerinfo.net/bioinformatics/category/webinar/).

Genetic Alliance webinars and resources

(http://beckerinfo.net/ bioinformatics/genetic-alliance/): Genetic Alliance "transforms health through genetics." They offer a large number of good resources for patients, caregivers, and clinicians on a host of genetic conditions. More about what they do: Leveraging the expertise of the genetics community builds capacity in our members through collaborative engagement. Genetic Alliance is at the crossroads of the genetics community.

Source: (http://beckerinfo.net/bioinformatics/category/webinar/).

NCBI Short Read Archive of NexGen Sequencing Data

(http://jeansong.wordpress.com/2009/08/19/ncbi-short-read-archive-of-nexgen-sequencing-data/): They are now maintaining the Short Read Archive (SRA) (http://www.ncbi.nlm.nih.gov/Traces/sra/) for parallel sequencing technologies. SRA allows you to :

- a) Search and display SRA project data through their homepage
- b) Search and display SRA project data through Entrez (http://www.ncbi.nlm.nih.gov/sra?term=all%5Bsb%5D)
- c) Download data through Aspera Connect (http://www.aspera.com/en/software-license-management/)
- d) BLAST service (http://blast.ncbi.nlm.nih.gov/Blast.cgi? PROGRAM=blastn&BLAST_PROGRAMS= megaBlast&PAGE_TYPE=BlastSearch&BLAST____SPEC=SRA) for sequence similarity searching of 454 sequencing reads for transcriptome studies

NCBI 3D Structure Help

(https://jeansong.wordpress.com/2009/08/ 05/ncbi-3d-structure-help/) : So the folks at NCBI have posted a whole bunch of useful help files on the web for their 3D structure resources, 3D Macromolecular Structure (http://www.ncbi.nlm.nih.gov/Structure/MMDB/docs/mmdb_ how_to.html) and Conserved Domains (http://www.ncbi.nlm.nih.gov/ Structure/cdd/docs/cdd_how_to.html). There are also other helpful how-to files which the fabulous Kristi Holmes over at Becker Library at Wash U has already blogged about here (http://beckerinfo.net/ bioinformatics/2009/07/29-3d-structure-help-from-ncbi/). Oh, there's a link to that blog, Bioinformatics@Becker (http://beckerinfo.net/bioinformatics/), in my blog roll in case you haven't already checked it out.

Social Networking

(https://jeansong.wordpress.com/2008/08/13/social-networking/) - A recent Information Week article describes social networking sites as growing so hopefully all of this blogging, twittering, flickering…is not in vain. Read the full article at (http://www.informationweek.com/ news/internet/social network/showArticle.jhtml?articleID= 210003458).

flickr

(https://jeansong.wordpress.com/2008/07/23/flickr/) : In case you are looking for images to use for your presentations and worry about copyright implications, flickr (https://www.flickr.com/) is a great resource for finding images that have a Creative Commons (http://creativecommons.org/) license so that you may use the image according to the CC licensing terms.

Blog roll

a) American Medical Informatics Association (http://www.amia.org/)

b) Bioinformatics@Becker (http://beckerinfo.net/bioinformatics/)

c) Center for Computational Biology and Medicine (http://www.ccmb.med.umich.edu/)

d) Kristiology (http://kristiology.blogspot.com/)

e) National Center for Integrative Biomedical Informatics (http://www.ncibi.org/)

f) Open Access News (http://legacy.earlham.edu/~peters/fos/fosblog.html)

g) PolITiGenomics (http://www.politigenomics.com/)

Chapter 6: BIOINFORMATICS IN SOCIAL MEDIA

(http://www.webicina.com/bioinformatics/news-and-information-on-
bioinformatics/#package_container)

Curated Social Media Resources
in Medicine & Healthcare!
Over 140 medical topics, 5000 resources, 20 languages.

Social Media

The number of communities and repositories dedicated to Bioinformatics is rapidly growing
so finding relevant resources takes more and more time and efforts. Webicina selected only
relevant social media resources for you. (Links for all items are shown)

 News

(http://www.webicina.com/ bioinformatics/news-and-
information-on-bioinformatics# package container)

blog (http://www.webicina.com/bioinformatics/ bioinformatics-in-the-
blogosphere#package_container)

 podcast (http://www.webicina.com/bioinformatics/
bioinformatics-podcasts-and-interviews# package container)

 community

(http://www.webicina.com/bioinformatics/ bioinformatics-community-sites-
facebook-groups-and-forums#package_container)

twitter (http://www.webicina.com/bioinformatics/ microblogging-twitter-and-friendfeed#package_container)

 wiki (http://www.webicina.com/bioinformatics/ bioinformatics-wikis#package_container)

video

(http://www.webicina.com/bioinformatics/ bioinformatics-videos-animations-and-videocasts#package_container)

 mobile phone (http://www.webicina.com/bioinformatics/ mobile-applications#package_container)

 search engine (http://www.webicina.com/bioinformatics/ medical-search-engines#package_container)

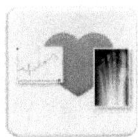 other resources (http://www.webicina.com/bioinformatics/ bioinformatics-resources#package_ container)

 slideshow (http://www.webicina.com/bioinformatics/ slideshows-about-bioinformatics#package_container)

Follow this category on	Share this page	Suggest a site
Submit	More Sharing Services Share| Share on favourites Share on face book Share on twitter Share on google_plusone_share Share on digg	Site URL: Submit

News and Information on Bioinformatics

There are more and more resource collections and networks focusing on Bioinformatics. Here are the best repositories of Bioinformatics-related information.

Bioinformatics-related medical blogs

In the huge cloud of Bioinformatics blogs, you will find hundreds of blogs containing spams and uncontrolled advertisements. Here we collected only the best blogs that have been providing quality information for a long time.

Bioinformatics Podcasts and Interviews

Patients like listening to quality interviews about Bioinformatics rather than reading such articles. We collected both the active and inactive podcasts.

Bioinformatics Community Sites, Face Book Groups and Forums

If you do a search for "Bioinformatics community" or forum in Google, you will find thousands of sites and also similar Face book groups, but the majorities of them have no relevance. On Webicina, we feature only the best Face book groups, applications, community sites and networks.

Micro-blogging: Twitter and Friend-feed in Bioinformatics

Sometimes it is easier to share messages and interesting links dedicated to Bioinformatics than writing blog entries or longer articles. Through micro-blogging, you can access relevant content in just seconds but only if you follow Twitter accounts of medical professional and empowered patients, patient communities, and book authors who write about Bioinformatics.

Bioinformatics Wikis

Wikipedia and medical wikis where only medical professionals can edit entries provide great content devoted to Bioinformatics.

Bioinformatics videos, animations and video casts

There are numerous useful video channels in Bioinformatics, but finding the best resources is really challenging. We have not only collected the most informative video channels but also interviews and animations.

Bioinformatics on Mobile

In Bioinformatics, mobile applications can have an important role such as facilitating collaboration, making new contacts or sharing pieces of advice.

Social Bookmarking in Bioinformatics

If you are looking for quality Bioinformatics links and resources, you can spend a lot of time and effort dealing with common search engines, but we only feature the most relevant collections.

Medical Search Engines in Bioinformatics

Google, Bing or Yahoo searches show you any kind of content from spams to advertisements. If you need only medically relevant information on Bioinformatics, here are medical search engines that search in selected content.

Slideshows about Bioinformatics

Many professionals upload interesting slideshows focusing on Bioinformatics and practical pieces of advice. We collected the most informative presentations for you.

Source: (http://www.webicina.com/bioinformatics/)

References

1. **1.**Altman R (1998) A curriculum for bioinformatics: the time is ripe. Bioinformatics 14: 549–550.
   o   View Article

   * PubMed/NCBI
   * Google Scholar
   2.Ranganathan S (2005) Bioinformatics education–perspectives and challenges. PLoS Comput Biol 1: e52. doi:10.1371/journal.pcbi.0010052.
   * View Article
   * PubMed/NCBI
   * Google Scholar
   3.Zauhar RJ (2001) University bioinformatics programs on the rise. Nat Biotechnol 19: 285–286. doi:10.1038/85758.
   * View Article
   * PubMed/NCBI
   * Google Scholar
   4.Ditty JL, Kvaal CA, Goodner B, Freyermuth SK, Bailey C, et al. (2010) Incorporating genomics and bioinformatics across the life sciences curriculum. PLoS Biol 8: e1000448. doi:10.1371/journal.pbio.1000448.
   * View Article
   * PubMed/NCBI
   * Google Scholar
   5.Pevzner P, Shamir R (2009) Computing has changed biology–biology education must catch up. Science 325: 541–542. doi:10.1126/science.1173876.
   * View Article
   * PubMed/NCBI
   * Google Scholar
   6.Wefer SH, Sheppard K (2008) Bioinformatics in high school biology curricula: a study of state science standards. CBE Life Sci Educ 7: 155. doi:10.1187/cbe.07-05-0026.
   * View Article
   * PubMed/NCBI
   * Google Scholar
   7.Neil Sarkar I (2010) Editorial: bioinformatics education in the 21st century. Brief Bioinform 11: 535–536. doi:10.1093/bib/bbq071.
   * View Article
   * PubMed/NCBI
   * Google Scholar
   8.Jungck JR, Donovan SS, Weisstein AE, Khiripet N, Everse SJ (2010) Bioinformatics education dissemination with an evolutionary problem solving perspective. Brief Bioinform 11: 570–581. doi:10.1093/bib/bbq028.

- View Article
- PubMed/NCBI
- Google Scholar

9.Pavesi G, Siccardi A, Viale G, Grazioli C, Tiziana Calciolari M, et al. (2008) Hedgehogs, humans and high-school science. The benefits of involving high-school students in university research. EMBO Reports 9: 208. doi:10.1038/embor.2008.25.

- View Article
- PubMed/NCBI
- Google Scholar

-------------------------END-----------------------------------